RAISED BEHIND

THE

TRIGGER

One father's journey to preserve our
outdoor heritage by teaching his
daughters how to hunt.

By Tim E. Hovey

Printed in the United States of America

For more information contact author at:

www.raisedbehindthetrigger.com
or
Timhovey4197@sbcglobal.net

Library of Congress Cataloging-in-Publication Data

Tim E. Hovey

Raised Behind the Trigger/Tim E. Hovey

p. cm.

ISBN: 978-0692684696

To Alyssa Nicole and Jessica Leigh:

I have taught you to be tough, compassionate, strong young women, with thoughts and minds of your own.

You have taught me so much more.

When I look at them, I have but one thought; you can't make fire feel afraid!

Table of Contents

PREFACE

When I first came up with the concept of documenting this journey, my initial thought was that the end product would be a guiding text for others; a simple outline of how my two daughters went from toddlers to hunters. However, as I began to write, the concept grew into something more important. During almost every outing with Alyssa and Jessica, I found new things to write about. As they got older and more inquisitive, they began to ask questions about all aspects of hunting.

I soon discovered that in the training of these two young hunters, I was being afforded a unique opportunity to watch how my two daughters viewed this activity. Their questions were fresh, innocent and came from a place of untainted curiosity. They weren't jaded by preconceived notions of hunters or hunting. Their inquiries were asked out of genuine interest. Not only were they slowly learning the intricacies of shooting and hunting, they wanted to know why our family hunted and others didn't.

Those early questions made me realize that a how-to guiding text on anything is essentially useless unless you provide reasons for why the subject matter is so important. Early on, it became just as vital for me to not only safely train my daughters, but to verse them on why passing on our hunting heritage was crucial to its continued existence.

Hunting is the most important resource management tool we have for correctly managing our valuable game species, and keeping those populations healthy for hunters and non-hunters to enjoy. Supported by over 150-years of science generated through following the principles of the North American Model of Wildlife Conservation, sportsmen are at the forefront of preserving our natural resources for future generations.

As sportsmen, we have an obligation to educate the misinformed in an effort to represent a true sportsman's heart. We should also make it a top priority to engage anyone, young and old, interested in learning about hunting. Knowledge is power and this has never been more evident than in today's volatile battle to preserve our outdoor heritage.

I believe the strongest weapon we possess to assure our heritage lives on is to pass this rich legacy to the next generation. Passing our knowledge and interest to our children will increase our ranks and spread our positive message, engaging young individuals in what man has done for tens of thousands of years. We are conservationists. We are hunters and we are not going away. What we do is important, valuable and is backed by over a century of science. We must forever appreciate our role and pass that interest on.

At the beginning of this journey the original plan was to expose my young daughters to shooting, and then to eventually take them hunting with me. I wanted them to experience the outside world and see why it had been such a powerful influence in my life. As they grew, I wanted us to sit at the edge of canyons as the sun came up and talk about life, and we have. During this time, I was sure that I'd have a front row seat to their blossoming confidence and overflowing self esteem, and I did. I wanted to build memories that each of us would treasure for the rest of our lives. Now, standing on this side and looking back, I realize it was so much more important than all that.

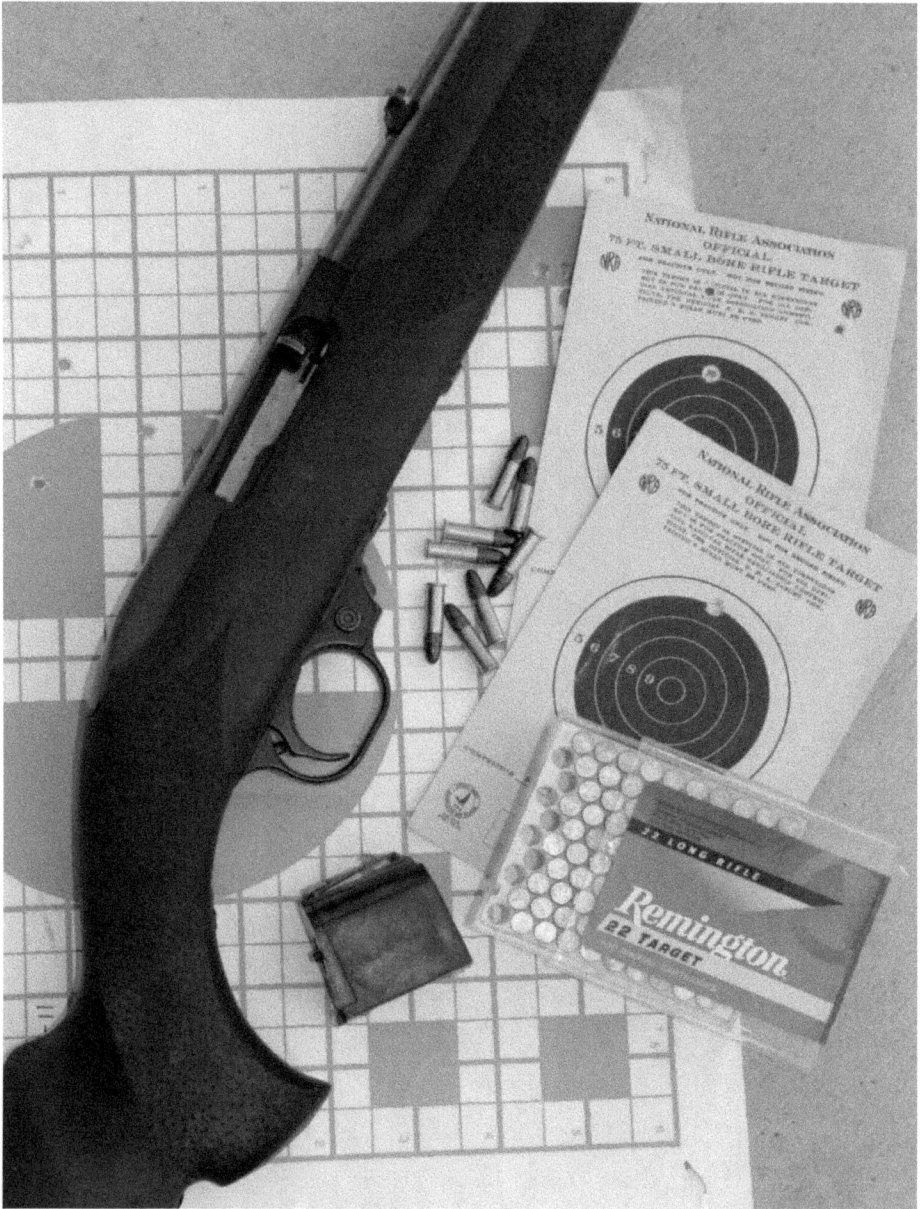

AWAKENING A HUNTER'S HEART

A few days after Christmas in 1976, I woke before everyone else, grabbed my brand new Crossman, single shot BB-gun and headed for the upper deck just off our living room. The elevated perch faced the front of the rural home, which sat on an acre of land. I eased the unlocked sliding glass door open and stepped out onto the frost-covered deck. Barefoot, I walked to the right side of the walkway quietly and knelt down, hiding behind the rail. The sun hadn't hit the front side of the house yet and the small patch of green lawn was still in the shadow of the home. Several dark brown mounds littered the lawn and looked like tiny foxholes of an encroaching enemy. I eased the barrel of the loaded air gun through the slats of the guard rail and lay down in the prone position on the frozen deck. It was cold, but I didn't care; I was there to hunt for the very first time.

I completely believe that I was born a hunter. I have a relatively large family and not a single one of those individuals was interested in the outdoors. Fishing and hunting trips were not a regular activity for our California clan and when I was young, I didn't know anyone that hunted. From a very early age, I knew that the interest was there. I also knew that if I wanted to explore that interest, I would have to do it on my own.

Early on, I would read every outdoor magazine that I could get my hands on. I educated myself on tips and tactics, and did everything I could to put fish on a stringer or game in the freezer. Without a mentor, I didn't have much success in those early years. It was a long road littered with almost constant failure. The one thing that eventually led to my gradual success was that I never gave up.

During my early exploring years, I would search our suburban backyard for lizards, snakes and frogs. At that time, it was all about the pursuit. I'd catch them, check them out and then release them. I learned quickly where the critters hung out and how to capture them.

At the age of twelve, my family moved to Atascadero, California, a rural community south of the town of Paso Robles. Our brand new house sat on an acre of undeveloped land, containing exactly one large oak tree. As soon as the truck was unpacked, I was out exploring my new territory. With the capture of my first ever horned lizard and a small king snake on our new property, I was in heaven.

Along with the slew of cold-blooded creatures, our new chunk of land was absolutely infested with gophers. New and old mounds littered the terrain like small, dirt volcanoes. On occasion, I would see the small mammals poking their small heads out of the ground, pushing dirt and always looking confused. For some reason I became obsessed with catching them. Within weeks of relocating to Atascadero, my dad became very supportive of my gopher-catching venture.

For reasons I am still unclear on, my parents tried to suburbanize a small section of the wild land at the front of our house. My mom began planting fruit tree seedlings in a careful pattern at the front of the parcel. My dad smoothed out a rectangular section of soil adjacent to the front walk way. Not having a single blade of green grass to mow, he wanted to establish a lawn in the front of our ranch house. You could almost hear the gophers giggling with joy.

Within a few weeks, the lawn had come in lush and green. A week after that, the gophers found it. With a shovel and a hose, my dad did his best to hold back the wild hoard. He'd jam the running hose down one hole and wait for the water to pop up in another. It was a futile effort that only served to anger my dad and soggy up the patch of lawn. He eventually gave up, or so I thought.

A few months later, packaged in identical boxes and wrapped under the Christmas tree were two, Crossman, single shot BB-guns. My brother and I were beyond excited and couldn't wait to get out and give them a try. Before the gift wrapping hit the floor, my dad made it clear that the guns weren't toys and we needed to put them to good use. Apparently the gifts came with special conditions. He stated that our first order of business was to thin out the subterranean herd in the front yard.

Using a raw potato and sniping from the upper deck, I practiced for a few days. I got to where I could hit the potato no matter where it was on the lawn. During my time on my improvised shooting range, I started to notice that every single morning new gopher mounds would appear on the green parcel. I knew if I wanted a chance to knock down the gopher numbers, I needed to wake early.

Early the next morning, I grabbed the gun and made my way to my elevated perch. I lay prone on the frost-covered deck and eased the barrel through the wooden slats. Two new mounds had appeared overnight and I traded my glance between each, waiting for movement. Within minutes of setting up, one of the mounds showed some activity. The dirt in the center began to move and within seconds the dark brown head of a gopher appeared, pushing the dirt to the edge of the mound. I moved the air rifle slightly, sighted down the barrel and squeezed the trigger. I saw the bb hit the rodent in the head and bounce off. For a second he just sat there. At first I thought I had killed him, but then he came out of the hole, looked around and then disappeared quickly below ground.

That was the first time I had ever fired a projectile at any live animal and it definitely had an impact on me. I could feel my heart beating strongly in my chest after the shot and a surge of excitement raced through my body. The gopher had escaped, but the idea of hitting a potato-sized object from thirty feet away with my trusty air rifle had changed me. I knew from that day on I would pursue any game that inhabited our little parcel of land with my Crossman.

I spent many years shooting lizards and small birds around our property with the Crossman. I used the air rifle so much that it eventually fell apart in my hands from overuse. Even at my young age, I knew that shooting little reptiles and non-game birds was just practice for actual hunting. I also understood the limitations of the air rifle. If I wanted to move on to bigger game, animals that I could actually eat, I needed to acquire an actual rifle.

Drawing off knowledge gathered from reading outdoor magazines, I decided that my next firearm should be a .22 rifle. I found an article that pictured a brace of fluffy rabbits artistically placed next to a bolt action .22. The article was filled with information on how to hunt with the small caliber firearm.

With a rehearsed speech and the article firmly in hand, I approached my dad with the rifle request. My dad had other ideas. He didn't have a lot of knowledge about the shooting sports, but he did understand the difference between the noggin-thumping air rifle and a true firearm in the .22 rim fire.

Over the next few months, I made several requests for a .22 rifle, but my dad wasn't budging. Sighting my young age and the expense, the acquisition of my first real rifle wouldn't come until years later.

Despite my gear limitations, I continued reading about the outdoors and learning all I could about hunting. During a summer camping trip, with my dad's approval, I was able to bring along a borrowed lever-action .22. I set up a target nearby camp and went through a box of ammo getting used to the rim fire. After adjusting to the Weaver scope on the older rifle and reassembling a few parts, I headed out to look for game.

At my side was our golden retriever runt, Pupdog. Born on the cold cement floor of our garage, and unnoticed for a few hours, she was the smallest of the litter. Ice cold when I found her, I figured she was dead. I scooped her up and started warming her in a towel. Within a minute, she started to squirm and whimper. Over the next few months, one thing became very clear; Pupdog was a survivor. What she lacked in size and overall retriever appearance, she made up for in general happiness and inexhaustible energy.

Pupdog raced ahead of me on a creek trail near an oak grove. I had seen ground squirrels moving through the banks of the small creek on the drive in. I figured I'd bring the dog to help spot game and she was always willing to head out on an adventure.

She ran out in front of me, sniffed a bush and continued running down the trail. When I walked by the same bush, a huge jackrabbit jumped out and ran up a small valley, disappearing into the thick vegetation at the top. For some reason, I knew that I was going to kill that hare.

Since she had failed to sniff out the rabbit, I took the dog back to camp and hiked back to the valley where I had last seen the jack. I looked the area over and spotted a young oak tree that would put me about 75-yards from the rabbit brush. I decided to stalk to that tree, sit down and wait for the rabbit to come back out.

Using some stalking tactics straight out of an old issue of Outdoor Life, I silently made my way to the oak tree and settled in. I sat at the base of the oak and rested my back against the tree. I shouldered the rifle and placed my elbows on my bent knees. I looked through the scope and easily spotted the area where I had last seen the jack rabbit. I got as comfortable as I could and waited. After all these years, I can still remember clearly that I was prepared to wait at the base of that tree all day.

About 45-minutes into the wait, I spotted a cottontail rabbit feeding up on the hill. I watched him through the scope and placed the crosshairs on his chest but didn't pull the trigger. Having never eaten rabbit, I had no idea that the cottontail would've been the better of the two species to eat. All I knew was that the jack was bigger and I was waiting for him.

After a few minutes, the cottontail fed his way back into the bushes. Not one minute later the big jack popped out of the thick cover. He walked out to a small opening and started feeding. My heart was thundering in my chest and I felt myself shaking. I moved the rifle slightly over and watched him through the scope. I slowly cocked the hammer back on the lever-action and watched the jack lift his head at the clicking sound.

The crosshairs danced on his shoulder briefly and I squeezed the trigger. At the shot, I watched the large jack flinch and then quickly escape back into the brush. That was the first shot I had ever taken at a game animal.

My heart thumped loudly for a minute after that. I wasn't sure I had hit the rabbit until I hiked up to the open area and saw a long stream of blood. I knelt down next to it and caught a glimpse of something in the brush. The dead jack rabbit sat ten feet from the blood in the dirt. My first hunted animal was laying there and I was beyond proud.

I grabbed the rabbit and laid it in the dry grass. I looked at the bullet wound and saw that it was exactly where I had aimed. I smoothed down the fur and felt a bit of sadness mixed with pure excitement. That moment on the hillside changed my life forever. I knew that I was a hunter and I knew that I would be involved in hunting for the rest of my life.

These two pivotal events were definitely the spark of interest that started my hunting career. I can remember everything about each episode and I think about how lucky I was to have discovered that interest. From then on, I continued educating myself about the outdoors and absorbed absolutely everything related to hunting.

When I purchased my first car at the age of seventeen, there was no stopping me in my outdoor pursuit. The following year, reaching the required age to purchase a firearm, I bought a Ruger 10/22. At the gateway of becoming an adult, all I wanted to do was head to the outdoors and hunt. I've known for most of my life that hunting was a part of me, and as mentioned, I strongly believe I was born this way.

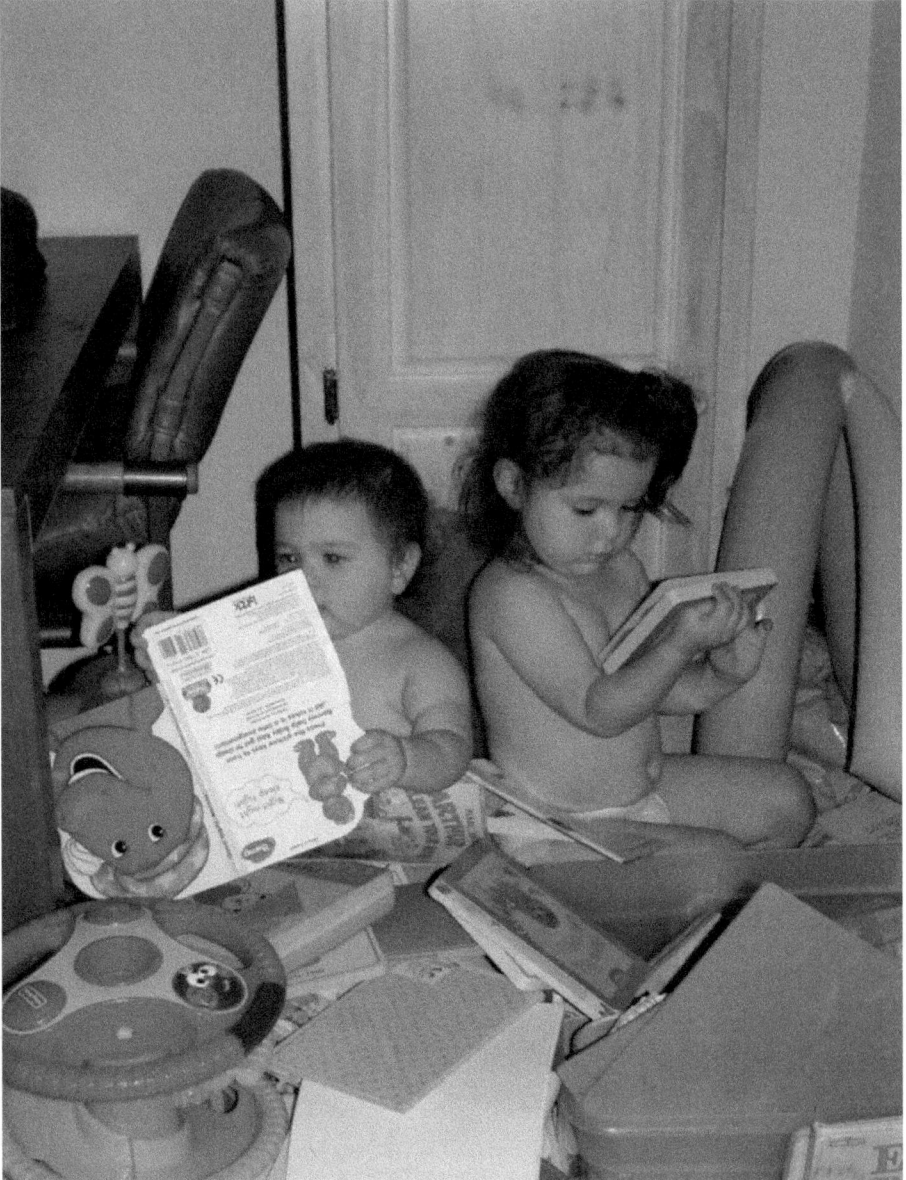

PASSING IT ON

Before the birth of my kids, I simply enjoyed hunting as much as I could, without much thought of educating others or passing it on. I don't really recall if there was anyone that was interested in learning from me during those early hunting trips. I either went by myself or sought out friends that also liked to hunt and we went when we could.

I now realize that in a time when our hunting heritage is being attacked constantly, endorsing the activity and getting others involved whenever we can is the true measure of a sportsman. To be perfectly honest, I wasted many years not getting others involved. As I got a bit older, I realized that participating in an activity that draws such a divisive line in the sand without endorsing it to the next generation was selfish. I decided to change all that a few months after my second daughter was born.

In the fall of 2000, my wife, Cheryl and I welcomed the birth of our first child, Alyssa Nicole. As new parents, we adjusted our lives to accommodate our new arrival, but we agreed that we'd gradually introduce our children to the activities we enjoyed. Alyssa was a daddy's girl from day one. Before she could walk, she would crawl over to me and fall asleep in my lap. Before her first birthday, she was already a veteran of two tent camping trips, comfortable sleeping in a portable crib under the stars.

In the spring of 2002 daughter number two, Jessica Leigh arrived to complete our young family. Jessica was a sturdy and mischievous baby that would greet you with the biggest smile as she smeared diaper cream all over her belly. She was curious, inquisitive and an absolute joy to be around. Her spring arrival lined her up for her first summer camping trip at just five months old. Just like her sister, she was eager to go anywhere we went.

Early on, it wasn't unusual to see a baby stroller outside our tent during camping trips. When my daughters reached the toddler stage, we took them fishing and on short hikes. Whenever we were outside as a family, we'd show them animal tracks and look for wildlife. When they reached the ages of five and seven, we spent a summer traveling the back hills of California looking for snakes. At the end of that adventure, both girls could identify any southern California species we encountered and they usually spotted snake tracks in the dusty road before I could.

I watched my girls grow in those early years with the pride of a new father. I watched their wonderment and enthusiasm blossom with every outdoor adventure, and early on, I was determined to teach them all I knew about the outside world. I knew when I was outside, my little girls would be right there with me.

This journey took the better part of eight years, and my daughters and I are still learning from each other. Now, at the gateway of their young adult lives, my daughters have become amazing shots, conscientious hunters and solid stewards of our natural resource. The path has not been an easy one and has been littered with fear, apprehension and frustration. Despite the obstacles, we stayed the course and never quit. We took this journey together, and I will always treasure that. I will forever believe that Alyssa and Jessica are better adjusted and kinder individuals for walking this path with me; I know I am. My daughters are now hunters, and this is how we got here.

Disclaimer

Before you read on, the following section needs to be expressed. I am by no means an expert on anything. In simple terms I am a hunter who likes to write. I have long been a firm subscriber to the phrase 'a Jack of all trades, a master of none.' With that said, the techniques and advice I present in this book are methods that have worked for me and my daughters during this journey. This text is intended to be used as nothing more than a suggested schematic of how to introduce individuals into the activity of hunting. Most of these tactics are practical and extremely obvious, but when I first set out to write this book, I wanted to be able to take the reader from not knowing the first thing about introducing others to hunting, to feeling comfortable at using this text as a guide to getting more individuals interested in the outdoors.

Topics like gun handling, gun safety, specific hunting techniques and safety equipment are presented in this text as advice only. Specific steps on how to guide beginners through the importance of all aspects of basic gun handling safety is up to the reader. The liability of training, instructing and informing novice sportsmen through this journey lies with the reader. I absolutely hate that this needs to be stated up front, but unfortunately, it is the world we live in today.

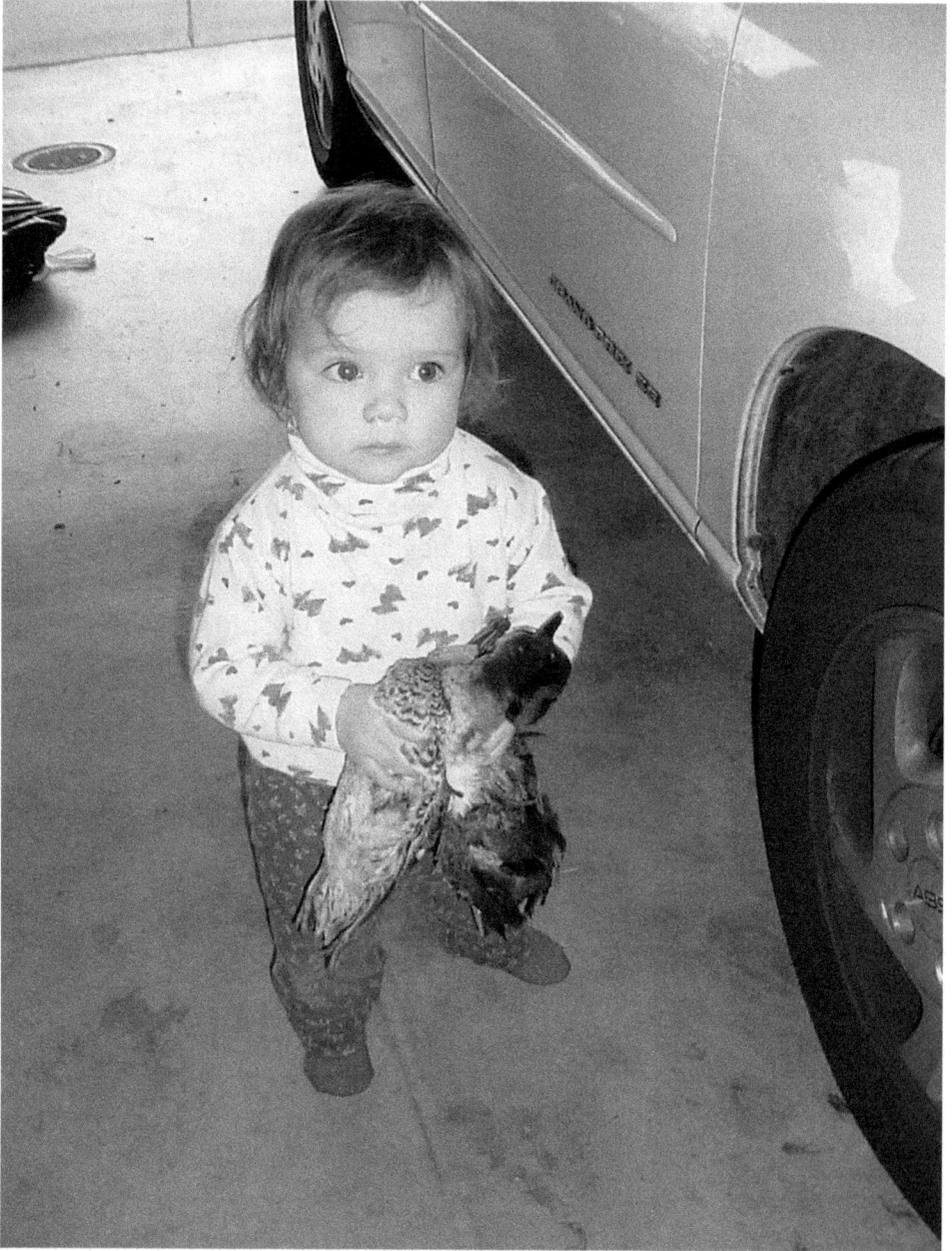

BEFORE THE FIELD

The groundwork for this journey began long before Alyssa and Jessica came out with me to shoot. From a very early age, we included the girls in all of our outdoor activities. Both my daughters were veterans of several tent camping trips by the time they were three and they were both very comfortable being outside.

During those early trips, both my wife and I made sure that when wildlife was seen, we'd discuss it as more than just a sighting. As a family, we'd talk about the animal's habits, where it lived and how it related to the overall ecosystem. Being biologists, we felt it was very important that the girls understood how all the animals, both predator and prey, interacted.

They understood that a rabbit seen at the edge of our campground in the early morning may fall prey to a coyote or bobcat later that same day. On a hike where both the girls were still toddlers, we watched a hawk drop into a field near our campsite. Within seconds, the raptor jumped from the ground and started flying back to its perch, a gopher snake firmly held in its talons. They've known for most of their lives that almost all wild animals are food for other animals and people.

With their basic ecosystem training underway, I decided to start talking to my daughters about hunting. They already knew I hunted, but by the time I returned from a trip, the game had already been skinned and processed out in the field. During a successful dove hunt with a couple of friends, I decided to hold off on cleaning the birds until I got home.

Meeting me at the back of the truck

Starting when the girls were just toddlers, I had them meet me at the back of the truck when I returned home from hunting trips. Whether I was successful or not, I made sure that when I came home, they were there to see how it went. I also began processing whatever I killed back at home so they could see the animals I hunted turned into the meat we ate. It didn't matter if it was big game or small game I wanted them to see the animals up close so they could start to see how hunting fit into our lives.

After a hunt, it really didn't matter what I brought home, we started to establish our own family tradition. If they were home and they heard me pull up, they'd meet me at the back of the truck to see how I had done.

In my opinion, this laid the ground work for their introduction into our family activity. Being from southern California, the hunting community is relatively small and very spread out here. The hunting activity is not as widely supported here as it may be in other states, so I was seriously the only example for them to look to. While most families out here were gearing up for weekend team sporting events, I was loading firearms into my truck before light and headed for the outdoors. If I wanted my girls to learn how to hunt, they were going to have to learn it from me.

Some of their first interactions with animals came on the tailgate of my truck at the end of a hunt. I would let them look the animals over, touch the fur or feathers and ask me anything they wanted about what they saw. I would always let them know that the hunted animal was going to be our dinner and that while we mostly buy groceries at the super market, occasionally we shopped outside.

The show and tell didn't end there. If there was meat processing to do and they wanted to see it, I would let them watch. I can remember bringing home a wild pig I had killed one afternoon. The quarters and back straps were in a large cooler and I wanted to clean them up and process them for the freezer. Alyssa was about five and she came out to see what I was doing. She was always interested in seeing what I had killed and she would sit out in the shop watching what I was doing.

This particular time she seemed intrigued with the size of the back quarters and asked how they would fit into the oven. I explained that all meat, whether wild or store bought, needs to be processed into parts that we can easily use. I grabbed one of the long back straps and showed her where the cut of meat was located on a photo of a pig. After trimming it down, I started cutting single portions off the long piece of meat. As the beautiful steaks started piling up, she walked over and looked at the pile of round, inch-thick cuts. "Daddy, this looks just like the meat in the store," she said. It was subtle, but the connection from a wild animal to the cooler to our plates was made.

After that, if Alyssa saw that animals needed to be processed after a hunt, she'd head over to the work cabinet, grab a set of over-sized gloves, fit them to her tiny hands and help wherever she could. With her added inquisitiveness, her countless questions and her little gloved hands poking at every part of the animal, it was an absolute guarantee that meat processing would take me twice as long as if I had done it by myself. That didn't matter to me. No matter how long it took, if they wanted to help, I'd let them.

If I had to state definitively where this outdoor journey started, I would have to say those early gatherings at the back of my truck are where the spark of their interest began. As expected, it was only a matter of time before they started asking if they could go with me.

The Disneyland effect

Young kids are sponges when it comes to information and if their eyes are open, they're gathering data and putting it to use quickly. As parents we like to think that our information and guidance is of the utmost importance to our kids. In reality, it is just another part of the endless train of stimulating data, good and bad, that they're receiving almost constantly.

One area that may have to be discussed is the complete disconnect between what kids see on television and what real life has to offer, especially in the wild animal world. In a constant stream of talking bears, clothes-wearing tigers and dancing snakes, kids start life early with a skewed sense of real animal behavior. As youngsters, they'll bring this misguided baggage with them into the outdoors unless you let them know the difference. As kids, they love their cartoons, and the stories and characters that these shows introduce them to. However, they need to understand that these shows are pretend and don't represent anything that actually exists.

I think the most damaging behavior that this type of programming instills in young minds, is that any animal they encounter is kind and approachable. I can remember when I was only seven years old, my younger brother saw a big male German Sheppard on our front yard, sniffing around a female beagle. My brother approached the larger dog, dropped down on all fours, and started barking at the male. The Sheppard turned on him, grabbed him by the face and shook him like a rag doll, leaving him with scars he has to this day. My brother likely learned that mimic behavior from a children's cartoon show that offered little in the way of proper canine etiquette when a large male dog is interested in a female. A far less violent example occurred years before I took my daughters out with me.

When Jessica was six and still way too young and immature to hunt with me, I would always show her the animals I had taken while hunting. I did this because Jessica seemed a little bit less interested in the outdoors than her older sister. I wanted to make sure I was providing her with the same interactions so that she could eventually make her own decisions on whether the outdoors was for her or not.

I had just returned from a successful predator hunting trip where I had called and killed two bobcat. I had loaded them into the garage and started preparing them to skin. Alyssa was already grabbing gloves to help me and she had pulled a small folding chair near the area to watch the show. Jessica, copying her big sister, dragged her Sponge-Bob Square Pants chair into the garage, set it next to Alyssa's and sat down. I had just hung the first cat, head down on my gambrel and was about to start cutting when I looked down and saw Jessica crying. I put down my knife and knelt next to her and asked her what was wrong. She looked up at me with soggy eyes and said, "I wanted to pet the kitties!"

After a brief discussion and showing her the long teeth and sharp claws of the bobcat, I helped her understand that wild animals are wild and would not let any human get close. Given her young age, I made sure I didn't spend a lot of time explaining the difference, but I felt it was important that she understood that the world of wild animals is not what she sees on television.

From that day on, I would make casual efforts to teach them the truth. During drives we would talk about all sorts of stuff, but when the topic came around to the outdoors and wild animals, we'd discuss the true facts about animal behavior, and the general panorama of the true wild kingdom.

Unfortunately, this gap in understanding regarding the true nature of wild animals does not end with children's cartoons, or children. Thanks to the nightly, feel-good stories about animal encounters on the evening news, even adults are guided down this path of misinformation.

I started to notice that almost nightly, our local evening news would slip in an animal story about fifteen minutes after the broadcast started. They appeared to run one of two regular themes; a human-wildlife interaction, that the news anchors always made cutesy and anthropomorphic, and some pet adoption piece that they placed before the four alarm church fire.

While I do own a dog, I don't believe advertising available pets is something that should be considered news. The combination of adorable puppies adorned with ribbons and the meaningless and often uneducated banter between the news anchors about the wild animal story is an overdose of cute that does nothing more than mislead the viewer. For many that aren't interested in the outdoors, this is where they get their animal information, and in my opinion, this can be dangerous. This news formula has a tendency to desensitize adults to the true demeanor of wild animals.

During a recent newscast, in the span of two hours, our local California news station ran these stories in the first twenty minutes of the broadcast. Prior to notifying the public about a body found in southern California, the news anchor reported on a puppy that had fallen down a narrow steel pipe and had to be hoisted out by the local fire department. The piece was littered with footage of the cute puppy being held by the heroic fire fighters after the rescue and then handed to a teary eyed, yet thankful young girl who was the dog's owner.

Staying on the animal theme, that story was followed by footage of a sow bear and her two cubs ripping through the garbage of a suburban neighborhood. The film clip showed the momma bear tipping over the large plastic trash container and grabbing a large bag of garbage, spilling its contents as she cut between two houses, her two cubs obediently following close behind. There was very little commentary during the clip until they cut back to the studio. Both anchors were hunched over the monitors smiling, genuinely enjoying the clip. One of them making a comment that the bears were just doing what bears do. The other anchor holding her hands to her face, saying, "Oh, I'd love to just take one of those cubs home." In the span of five seconds, one had stated misinformation on true wild bear behavior, and the other had offered up a desire to own a wild animal that she knew absolutely nothing about.

Finally, a little later in the newscast, they covered a story where a family in a different country had adopted two lion cubs, letting them live in their home along with their five small children. The clip showed the five small kids playing with the lion cubs, both weighing about 40-pounds apiece. One of the children was prodding the cubs with a broom, smiling as one of the cats grabbed the end tugging at it. I watched the clip, fully convinced that the kid with the broom would probably be the first to be mauled.

These types of stories do absolutely nothing to educate the public on true animal interactions. In fact, these brief news pieces, in my opinion, do more harm than good. These nightly feel-good pieces blur the line between humans and animals.

I believe those that know about the outdoors, understand it the best. Most sportsmen have grown up hunting, fishing and camping, me included. Through these activities, we have all developed an understanding of what wild animals can do and how we should interact with them.

I often used these misguided news reports as talking points with Alyssa and Jessica. I'd let them know that wild animals shouldn't be digging around in people's trash and certainly shouldn't be considered house pets. As a biologist, I made it a point to properly educate them on animal behavior and to correct any misinformation they may have picked up. By the time they were seven and eight, they both knew wild animals were wild, and they don't sing songs to us or wear pants.

Using your television for good

For the most part, I believe your television is a general time waster and a huge generator of misinformation when it comes to what we do outside. However, some of today's programs have actually assisted in helping my daughters see the difference. Another good method for introducing youngsters to more realistic wild animal behavior is viewing nature shows. I grew up watching these types of shows. I can still remember Mutual of Omaha's Wild Kingdom, and how Marlin Perkins would always stay safely in the studio while his associate, Jim would be out in the field, smiling obediently while getting mauled by an anaconda.

Back then, there wasn't much to choose from when it came to educating anyone on wild animals. Today is quite different. Several channels are dedicated to wild animal programs and most have updated their life history data to reflect recent science. These channels are excellent for introducing young viewers to relatively normal wild animal behavior without traumatizing them too much.

Once the kids get a bit older, and you think they're ready to see how hunting really unfolds, start showing them the programs aired on the Outdoor Channel. I believe all kids are different when it comes to their individual sensibilities at viewing hunts on television. I started letting both my daughters view some of the shows with me about the time they started coming out shooting with me. Understanding that these shows tend to represent snapshots of actual hunts, they do provide enough information so that young minds can grasp the concept of hunting.

I started the girls off watching upland bird hunting first. I did this for a very specific reason. The bird hunting shows often showed bird dogs anxiously sniffing the ground looking for quail. Once on point, the hunters got into position and flushed the hidden covey. Escaping birds were shot as they fly and at distance. The viewer is aware that the birds are killed, but the nature of this type of hunting

19

allows the viewer to be separated from the actually killing. I wanted the first hunting shows the girls viewed to be somewhat tame. I also wanted them to see how the bird dog worked with the hunter and how instrumental the well trained, domesticated animal was in assisting. They'd see the dog head out and retrieve the downed bird, and quickly bring it back to the hunter. In my opinion, this gave my daughters an example of how our pets and wild animals are completely different.

As they became more interested and older, we started watching all sorts of hunting programs together. Some of the big game shows actually showed the field dressing and processing of the animal at the end of a hunt. This not only looked familiar to what I did when animals came home with me, but it illustrated how much work was involved in processing a big game animal after the shot was taken.

Over the last few years I've been very pleased to see that some networks outside the Outdoor Channel have decided to air both hunting and trapping as an essential way of life in the deep wilderness. Shows like, Life Below Zero, Alaska, The Last Frontier and The Last Alaskan have all graphically depicted how life near the arctic circle is entirely dependent on what residents can kill themselves. There are no stores, butcher shops or meat sections where these people live. These shows provide great examples of how a different segment of society lives and interacts with wildlife, and how that wildlife is absolutely vital to their survival in the form of food and clothing.

I still believe that if we all unplugged our televisions tomorrow, we'd be better off for it. However, if you're selective on what your children watch with regards to the outdoors, I think you'll find good examples of what they can expect when they finally venture outside with you.

Let them participate in the wet work

Even before my daughters got behind the trigger, they were helping me process any wild game I would bring home. Before she knew what hunting was, Alyssa was helping me pluck geese in the garage. When they got to the toddler stage and I knew they were interested, I would keep whatever I killed chilled and wait to process it at home in front of them. I've always thought it was very important for Alyssa and Jessica to see how a hunted animal is turned into the meat we ate.

I remember one trip where I came home with a limit of mourning dove after an evening hunt. I put the birds on ice and decided to clean them with Alyssa's help. At home, I laid out some newspaper on the freezer, hoisted Alyssa up on the cooler so she could lend a hand and started breasting out the birds. After I cut the breast out, I handed the meat to Alyssa and she would carefully lay them out on a paper towel. She was almost three years old and after we were finished with one dove, she would reach into my game bag and grab the next one. We had our own little wild animal processing line going.

Once we were finished, I cleaned everything up and we walked into the house, Alyssa leading the way. She walked in and proudly stated, "Hey mom, we've got birdie meat for dinner!" After that, whenever I returned from a dove hunt, she would ask me if I brought home any birdie meat.

Measure their maturity

Since Alyssa is eighteen months older than her sister Jessica, I decided that I'd start taking her out target shooting first. A few weeks after her seventh birthday, we loaded the truck with a few rifles and headed out for her first ever shooting trip. I had gone over basic firearm safety with her at home and I felt like she was mature enough to understand that shooting was fun, but serious.

I can still remember getting a lot grief from my family for even considering taking her out shooting at such a young age. However, I consider myself a very protective father and I knew that Alyssa was mature enough to understand what we were doing.

In my mind, taking my seven-year old daughter out to shoot guns all hinged on Alyssa's maturity level. If I felt that she was still too young to understand the concept, and how serious it was, I wouldn't have taken her. Conversations with my wife confirmed that we both felt she was ready.

Maturity levels are as different as personalities. Some kids mature sooner in their thinking and understanding than others. When my youngest daughter, Jessica turned seven I knew that she wasn't quite ready to come out with me yet. She had a shorter attention span at that age and at that time, I wasn't even sure if she was interested in heading outdoors. I decided to let her make the call on when she wanted to come out shooting with me. With the exception of a disastrous early first trip, this turned out to be the right approach. Just shy of her tenth birthday, Jessica decided that she wanted to start shooting.

I can emphatically state that making the decision to use maturity level rather than age as a measure of preparedness was probably the most important decision of this entire process. If I had pushed Jessica at the age of seven to go from tagalong to shooter, she would've probably gotten frustrated and turned her back on the entire idea. It never really mattered to me if they wanted to participate or not. If they decided after that first shooting season that it wasn't for them, I would've completely understood. I did want to make sure that I was being fair to both girls in the amount of exposure to this new activity they were each receiving. Once they determined they were ready on their own, I was excited to move them to the next level.

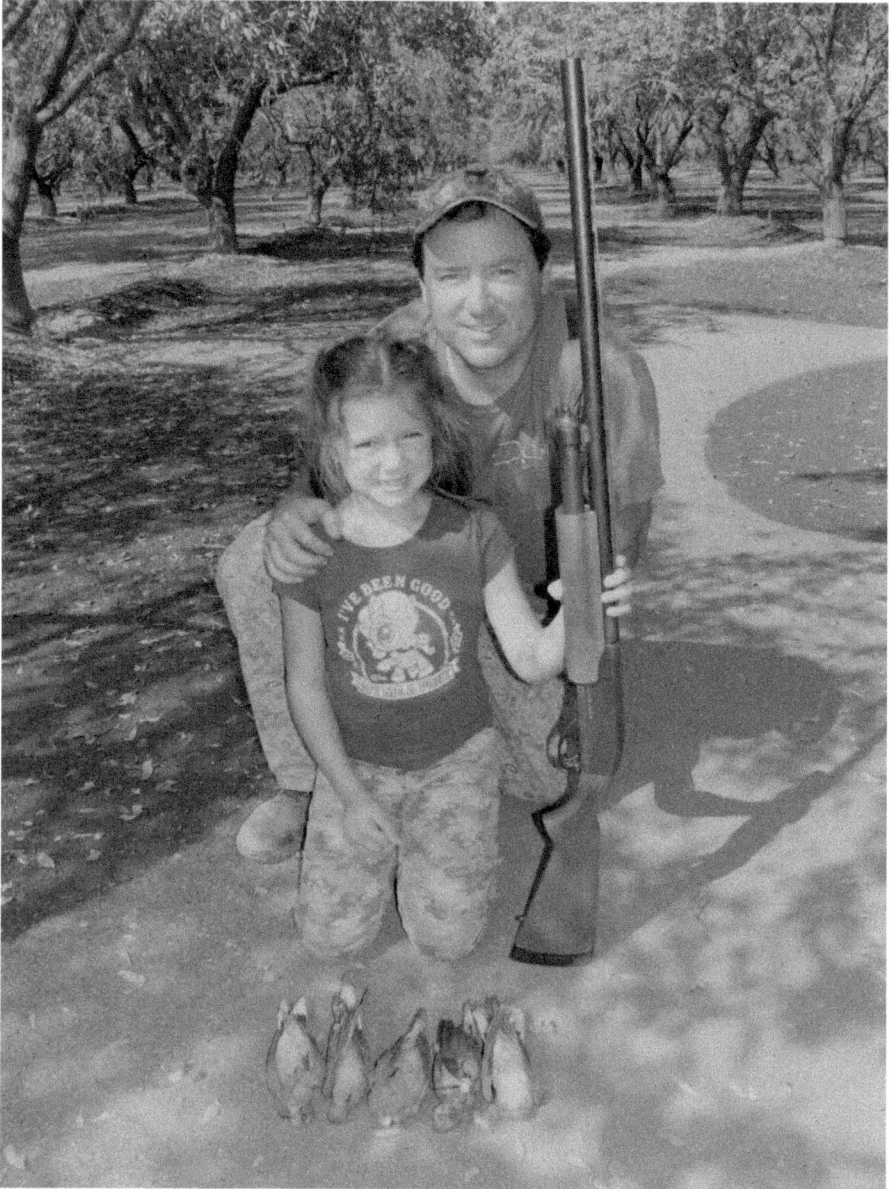

IN THE FIELD

In the fall of 2007 I began to plan the next level of training for my daughters. Alyssa had been interested in the outdoors from the beginning. Whenever I returned home from a trip, she was always the first to meet me in the driveway to see how I had done. She'd help me unload my gear and always wanted to help in the game processing. Every once in a while, she'd ask me when she could go with me.

I had shown her some of the basics of the .22 rifle she'd be starting with, and she had already started training in firearms safety. She knew that guns were tools that needed to be respected and handled correctly. With every solo trip home, she became more anxious to come with me. As a father, I wanted to make sure she was ready, but I also kept wondering what I was waiting for. A few weeks after her seventh birthday, I knew it was time to take her shooting. It was time for Alyssa to take that first real step towards becoming a hunter.

Alyssa's first trip

On my first drive out to the shooting area with Alyssa, I was extremely nervous. This was our first trip out together, just the two of us, and I can still remember feeling anxious during the entire drive. The spot I had chosen was located 90-minutes away in the Mojave Desert. I wanted an open area where we could practice alone and I knew the area well. I had made this trip myself dozens of times and I had never felt such anxiety. However, on this trip, I had my first born child with me and I obviously wanted to make absolutely sure she stayed safe out in the stark desert terrain.

There are lots of reasons no one lives in the desert. It's hot, it's desolate and it's full of rattlesnakes. There are rocky crags that are unstable, the dirt two-tracks can be impassable and dangerous, and if you get stuck, your cell phone would be about as helpful as a sandwich. I had always prepared for a time when I'd need to hike out to a main road, or somehow attempt to get help if I broke down. Every scenario I came up with involved a long hike in less than favorable conditions. In my mind, that was not a safe option for a seven-year old girl.

I guess it goes without saying that I did not take this next step in the training process lightly. During every trip out to shoot or hunt with my daughters, we left the driveway prepared. My truck contained ten gallons of water, a shovel, a small portable compressor, a tow strap and a GO kit that had a blanket, some snacks, matches and a flash light in it. The spare tire was always checked and a map of our location was always left behind so someone knew where we were headed and when we'd return. When we were out, I stayed on the good roads and didn't take any unnecessary chances. I wasn't paranoid, just cautious.

Be prepared

I discovered early on that adjustments would need to be made when I began shooting with my daughters. At times, when I was out hunting hard by myself, all I needed was some water and maybe a snack or two. I'd hit the desert at sun up and spend the entire day shooting and hunting with little more than a handful of food and water. While the heat did drain me, I could take it and often pushed myself to the very edge of comfort. During that very first trip with Alyssa, I realized that I would need to cater these trips completely to the girls.

Along with the standard safety provisions, I'd also add a cooler full of food, juice boxes and snacks. A couple of pillows and a blanket were tossed in the back seat so the girls could sleep during some of the longer drives. I also had a spare set of clothes and shoes for them in case they needed to change during our outings. Hats, sunscreen and lip balm were always present in the center console.

While I was absolutely certain I had all the supplies loaded, Alyssa made it clear during our first trip that I hadn't thought of everything. Twenty minutes after arriving at our shooting spot, and after her third juice box, she informed me that she had to pee. Luckily a five-gallon bucket that just happened to be in the back of the truck solved the problem.

After a few trips we figured out all the gear and supplies we'd need for a day out and I had it packed the evening before each trip.

I eventually overcame the uneasiness of taking the girls out to wild places. In the beginning, I just wanted to make sure they were safe. As the trips piled up, I realized that unnecessary worrying was a waste of time. I also understood that it was important to loosen the reins and let them run wild just like my parents had done for me. The ultimate goal from the beginning was to concentrate on having fun and building memories.

Safety gear

As a lifelong shooter and hunter, and having essentially taught myself the ins and outs of the outdoors, I didn't always use the safety gear when I should've. I didn't start using hearing protection until much later in life, and I'm kind of paying for that now. I did wear eye protecting in the form of sunglasses when I hunted, but my adherence to shooting safety gear was extremely loose in my early years.

Determined to lead a good example and keep the girls safe, I picked up a set of Walker's Game Ears for all of us. From the very beginning, both my daughters got used to wearing them just about every time we went shooting. In all honesty, there were times when they shot the .22 where they didn't always use them, but when I transitioned them to larger calibers, I made sure they always had their Walkers on.

Safety glasses or smaller sized sunglasses were always part of the packed gear as well. They quickly got used to using them when we were out target shooting, and while they didn't always wear them, I made sure they did when I noticed they were missing.

I also made sure that my daughters were wearing the appropriate attire when we were out exploring. Long sleeved shirts and heavy pants were mandatory when the truck was headed to the desert. Since we had started to develop a tradition of hiking rugged areas near our shooting spot, street clothes, shorts and flimsy shirts were left at home. My daughters also had high-ankle hiking boots that were the standard foot wear for our days out together.

Other items I included for trips out shooting were a pair of first aid kits. I had one that had the standard bandages, band aids and anti-itch creams in it. The other was more substantial and contained items that would be helpful for larger wounds. Add in my wilderness first aid training, and I felt like we were well prepared for anything that might arise. Thankfully, with the exception of a couple of band aids, nothing else out of the kits was ever used.

Understanding the necessity for hearing and eye protection, it's important to make sure your kids stay safe. With today's technology it's easy to set them up with the proper safety gear. Use the safety equipment from the beginning and it will become a natural part of the entire process. A good pair of hiking boots and a dedicated set of outdoor clothes will complete the outfit and make your kids feel like they're starting to accumulate their own gear for the outdoors. First aid kits take up little room and should be at the top of your safety gear list. We never really had to use ours, but I was always glad they were there. I'm required to stay trained in wilderness first aid for my job, and I feel that this training was a definite benefit when we're headed out to wild places. If you can find a place that offers a simple first aid class, or a focused class on wilderness first aid, I would highly recommend acquiring this training.

Here's a simple list of everything we'd take when we were headed out to shoot or hunt. I kept this gear in a medium-sized plastic tote so that everything stayed together and it was easy to load when we planned trips.

Safety gear
Hearing protection (Walker's Game Ear)
Shooting Safety glasses or high quality sun glasses
First aid kits (standard and advanced)
Tow strap
Shovel

Water jug
Blankets
Flashlight
GPS
Portable Air Compressor
Rope
Knife
Matches

Standard Necessities
Sunscreen
Hats
A spare set of clothes and shoes (jackets and sweatshirts)
Pillow and sleeping blanket
Toilet Paper
A five gallon bucket
Paper towels
Trash bags
Bottled water
Snacks (small granola or energy bars)
Food cooler (lunch supplies)

Temper the pace

Taking a child anywhere rugged is a challenge. As hunters, we're used to getting a little banged up on trips, and maybe extending our comfort zone in the heat of the moment. When young kids start making trips out with you, you'll need to temper the activity to their pace.

In the beginning, I'd let Alyssa and Jessica decide on what they wanted to do and how long they wanted to do it. This meant that a 90-minute drive could result in twenty minutes of shooting and then a little goofing off before we headed back. To keep the kids comfortable and entertained, I accepted this early format.

As they got a bit older, I changed things up. I made sure they knew that when we were headed out to shoot or hunt, we could possibly be out all day. Having them set the pace when they were new to the activity was fine, but once they were used to it, I started setting the pace.

Towards the end of our first shooting season, Alyssa and I actually started to develop a tradition during our shooting outings. We'd head out early and always grab breakfast on the road. She absolutely loved this. Once we arrived at our shooting area, I'd set up targets and let her shoot for as long as she wanted. If she wanted to take a break, I'd pick up the .22 and shoot for awhile. Once the shooting was done, we'd pack up our gear and drive around exploring.

We'd drive the desert roads looking for wildlife and checking out new areas. I used this time to identify new spots to hunt predators and small game. It also gave me an opportunity to locate spots where the terrain would be easier for kids to hike.

Around lunch time, we'd pull off in a shaded area and sit on the tailgate and eat. I'd point out canyons and spots I had hunted in the past, and we'd talk about when she'd be ready to hunt with me. Those tailgate lunches are some of my favorite memories.

In the early trips, I made sure I tempered the pace for both Alyssa and Jessica. I wanted them to enjoy the outings, but I didn't want to burn them out. Letting them set the pace during the early trips was definitely the right thing to do. However, after a handful of trips, I started letting them know that we'd be out a little longer each time to make the drive worth it. I felt like extending the trips gradually expanded their tolerance for spending more time out in the field.

Starter rifles

That first trip out I packed my Ruger .22 semi-auto rifle and a Steven's single shot .22. The Steven's is an open sight rifle and the Ruger is fitted with a Bushnell scope. Both are easy to handle and I wanted Alyssa to shoot each rifle so she could experience the different sighting options, and the difference between a bolt action and a semi-automatic rifle.

Even though both rifles were relatively light, Alyssa wasn't strong enough to safely support the full weight of the firearms while shooting. To keep her from getting fatigued, I set up a shooting bench and a rifle sled so that she could shoot for as long as she wanted without getting tired.

I set up a few targets out at about thirty yards and we got started. I shot the Ruger first so she could get an idea of the sound of the .22 and the slight recoil. I gave her some brief instruction and showed her how to mount up behind the rifle. We practiced looking through the scope and I explained how the crosshairs worked. I put a few bullets in the rotary clip and showed her how to load it. She positioned herself behind the Ruger and took her first shot.

For the next hour Alyssa fired at every target I set out. She quickly got the hang of adjusting to the scope and moving the bulky set up to fire on new targets. I could see instantly that she enjoyed the challenge of finding her target, getting it in the scope and making the shot. From that very first trip, I could see that Alyssa had the interest and the ability to become a proficient shooter.

The .22 rifle is a great starter rifle for kids. They're lightweight, easy to use and still relatively cheap to shoot. They are perfect for teaching young shooters the basics of aiming and squeezing the trigger. They are easy to operate and have almost no noticeable recoil. Their effective range is less than 100-yards, making them perfect for building confidence in young shooters that like to break targets inside that range.

That first trip was the first and last time Alyssa used a shooting bench during our target shooting sessions. On subsequent trips, I moved her to a shooting chair and a set of shooting sticks. Anyone can shoot well from a bench, but after her introduction to target practice, I wanted her using the tools I use when I hunt.

Before our second trip, I purchased Alyssa her own Cricket, single shot rifle in hot pink. This youth rifle had a secondary safety and was light enough for her to fully support during target practice. I also wanted her to have a dedicated piece of gear that was exclusively hers, instead of always using my firearms.

When it was time to start shooting, I always made sure I was focused on Alyssa. Whenever she was behind the trigger, I made sure I was there supervising. I kept a close eye on safety and continually stated the safety tips. The more I repeated them, the more I felt like they wouldn't forget them. Even now, years after they've been trained, I'm always reminding them about safety.

Getting comfortable with the basics

Within a few target practice sessions, both girls became proficient at shooting rifles. At first I let them use the comfort of small folding chairs and shooting sticks to shoot targets. I wanted them to get comfortable at the mechanics of looking through a scope, acquiring a target and gently squeezing the trigger. In my opinion, these are the fundamentals of shooting and where I was convinced we should start.

Making them comfortable in the beginning was the key for me. The reason for the chair was not only obvious, but served as a positioning tool during our target sessions. If you tell a child to sit down on the ground and get ready to shoot, chances are you'll be pulling and tugging on them until they get into the correct shooting position. With the small folding chair, I would place it in the exact area I wanted them to be and rotate it slightly right to accommodate their dominant hand. Before any other piece of gear was brought out, I knew they were in a safe area because I placed them there in the chair.

Using a set of shooting sticks or a rest of some kind is a great tool for teaching young kids how to shoot. Even some of the starter firearms are a bit front heavy for youngsters. Having the bulk of the rifle weight supported by the shooting sticks will keep your kids from getting tired and will help steady their shot. This of course will assist in accuracy and seeing themselves hit targets consistently will definitely increase their enjoyment of the activity.

In the beginning, I taught my daughters the same shooting stick technique that I use. Most rifles have a sling post on the front and back of the rifle. To give new shooters added stability, I had both my daughters place the rifle on the shooting sticks so that the front sling post was in front of the shooting stick support. This keeps the rifle from sliding backwards off the sticks when the rifle barrel is pointed up. I do this myself in hunting situations and it not only aids in shooting stability, it gives me a repeatable point where my sticks and rifle come together. When I need to move the set up quickly, I can firmly grip the set up at this junction and move rifle and sticks left or right of my position with ease.

Using the shooting sticks also served a safety purpose for us as well. When the girls were reloading or waiting for their turn, the rifles were secured on the sticks and positioned in known locations.

In almost all rifle hunting situations, I use a set of shooting sticks to steady my shot. I wanted this piece of equipment to become integral to my daughters' hunting future so I introduced it early in the process. Within a few trips they became comfortable using them and I believe being comfortable is key to making good shots in hunting situations. I consider myself a pretty good hunter and I was hoping that introducing specific pieces of gear that had brought me success would eventually translate into hunting success for them.

Types of targets

It's important to keep things interactive and exciting when you introduce kids to target shooting. Kids will quickly grow tired of punching holes in paper if that's all there is to shoot at. Today's target technology and variety should be used to keep kids entertained and interested.

From the start, I would bring along a box of clay targets whenever we went shooting. The girls loved breaking them with the .22 and would often go after these targets before any others. I quickly discovered that when it came to target shooting, my daughters liked to see stuff get knocked over or break. Soda cans filled with dirt, water bottles filled with sand and spent shotgun shells that could be set up and knocked down were all quick, easy and cheap targets for most trips.

Small caliber spinning targets and metal plates are also great options for kids. New shooters can get the instant satisfaction of hearing their shot hit metal or watching a target spin. One of our favorite targets was a large metal hanging plate set out at about 75-yards. The girls loved dinging the six-inch plate, and would at times empty an entire clip ringing the metal disc.

Once the girls got older and really got into being precise in preparation for hunting, I started using the See N Shoot targets. These targets show the bullet impacts in a highly visible color so we could get instant feedback on their shot placement. We'd often use these targets right before a hunting trip so we could refine their aim and to make sure the rifles were zeroed.

To keep recreational shooting fun and interactive for the kids, I strongly suggest that you include several different kinds of targets. Kids love seeing stuff break or things tip over after they shoot. You can also sharpen their skills by setting targets further out or placing smaller ones in with the others. Mixing things up a bit and challenging your kids with different types of targets will make them better shots.

Stepping up in caliber

During that first year, Alyssa shot over a thousand .22 rounds. She really enjoyed plinking with my Ruger semi-automatic rifle, and it was the first firearm she'd grab when we were out. She used her Cricket rifle for a few trips, but the single shot loading and the cheap scope left a lot to be desired. It was light enough for her to support, but she quickly adapted to loading and shooting the Ruger and preferred that rifle over the Cricket.

This small caliber is also ideal for a youngster's first hunting firearm. While limited in range, it's perfect for small game and introducing children into the hunter's guild. Most hunters started their hunting careers with the small rim fire, and even today, I don't know too many outdoorsmen and women that don't enjoy plinking with a .22. When they're old enough to hunt, start them off with this popular and reliable round and watch the excitement as they begin to bring home game. Truth be told, I re-discovered the enjoyment of shooting my .22 rifles when I began teaching Alyssa how to shoot.

During Alyssa's very early training, I also considered letting her use other small, recently introduced calibers like the .17 HMR. This rim fire cartridge is faster and more accurate than the .22, but the ammo is more expensive. For this reason I decided to stay with the .22 and save the faster rim fire for when Alyssa transitioned over to hunting. I had no issues with her shooting other calibers, but for economic reasons, her early training centered on the .22.

Once Alyssa got a little older and was comfortable shooting the smaller rifle, I started bringing larger calibers out for her to shoot. I have several rifles chambered in what I consider to be intermediate calibers. I do a great deal of predator hunting and have rifles chambered in .223, 22-250 and .204. These intermediate center fire cartridges are perfect transition calibers for kids already used to shooting the .22. These larger cartridges introduce new shooters to an increasing level of recoil and will prepare them to move up to true big game calibers.

I think it's very important to do this step-wise increase in recoil so kids can understand that as the cartridges get bigger, so does the recoil. Alyssa understood this, and was eager to try any caliber I brought out with us. Even though she was enthusiastic, I wanted to make sure she was ready and I didn't want to rush her progression.

Just before Alyssa's ninth birthday, she started shooting the .204. She adjusted to the stronger recoil within a few shots easily and started asking about larger calibers. Her transition to these intermediate calibers was seamless and within one trip she had shot all three of my predator rifles.

Alyssa was well aware that the new rifles she had graduated to were the same ones I used to hunt predators. She knew that adding these new calibers to her growing experience meant that as soon as she was old enough to get her hunting license, she could come predator hunting with me.

Using these .20 caliber center fire rifles to introduce children to the next level of recoil is a great way to wean them off the starter rifle. The recoil of these calibers is more noticeable than the .22, but easily manageable for young shooters. Getting them comfortable on the intermediate calibers will begin to prepare them for the big game calibers, increasing their hunting potential.

Transitioning young kids to larger calibers

You definitely need to be aware of your child's mass when you consider moving them up to larger calibers. One thing you don't want to do is move them to larger firearms before they're ready. Nothing can dampen a kid's enthusiasm faster than being afraid or apprehensive of getting pounded by more recoil than they can handle. Despite their eagerness to transition up to larger firearms, make very sure you consider their smaller frames before moving them up.

As they became comfortable with smaller calibers, I found that moving them up in a step-wise fashion worked well for us. I also let them make the call when they wanted to move up. I would make subtle suggestions that if they wanted to hunt larger game they needed to shoot larger calibers. Conversely, I remained the decision maker when my daughters wanted to graduate to the next level before I thought they were ready. Alyssa was asking to shoot the larger 30-06 before I thought she was big enough to absorb the recoil. I was impressed with her desire to experience more in the shooting world, but I didn't want to have that first big caliber experience be a bad one.

Both my daughters spent a few years shooting the .22 rifles and the other .20 calibers before I felt they were ready to move up. I used common sense and basic physics to decide when they were ready. As they got bigger, I knew they would be able to absorb the stronger recoil of my .30 caliber rifles far better than if they were smaller.

For obvious reasons both my daughters were a bit apprehensive at moving to the large calibers. While I understood their reservation, I had a hard time relating to their fear. To ease them into it, I reminded them that they already knew exactly what to expect when it came to recoil. I told them that the bigger caliber rifles wouldn't catch fire, bite them or do anything unexpected. It was simply a larger recoil punch than they've previously experienced. That's all.

To ease the recoil a bit during their first big caliber attempt, I set my daughters up on shooting sticks so that the front rifle sling post was positioned in front of the V of the sticks and right up against the support. As right handed shooters, their left support hand would grasp the sticks high, close to where the rifle rested. This allowed some of the recoil to be suppressed a bit with this set up.

Both my daughters eventually conquered their apprehension over the increased recoil. Alyssa moved through with a deep breath and half a box of ammo. Jessica took a bit more convincing, but it eventually became a non-issue.

Be patient and don't push too hard on your kids to conquer the next-level recoil. I found that if I just eased them into it and occasionally brought it up, they eventually got through it.

Let them help

As a father of two young daughters, early on I found that it was really difficult for me to relinquish any control during trip planning, gear gathering and set up. As parents, we want to do everything we can for our kids to make activities comfortable. In the beginning, I would load up the truck with all our gear, set them up at our target spot or hunting area, and essentially be the guide. When they were first starting out, I found it far easier and faster to take care of everything. As they progressed and got older, I started to notice that they continued to expect this special treatment and it wasn't getting any easier for me.

I can remember the day I realized that I had done too much. We had finished a nice day of target shooting and I was gathering the gear, folding up the shooting table and picking up trash. I looked over and saw Alyssa leaning against the truck watching. She was nine at the time and fully capable of assisting. I looked over and started handing out tasks. She instantly kicked into action and started helping out.

I take full responsibility for not getting her completely involved sooner. I realized that I hadn't gradually involved her in the planning and preparation of our adventures. I'd even give her the same canned response over those early years when she had started asking to help. Without hesitation, I'd state, "that's alright, I've got it." By taking total control I was cheating her out of participating in all aspects of preparation, and over burdening myself. If I wanted my daughters to truly understand everything about the outdoors, they needed to get their hands dirty.

My daughters needed to be a part of the entire process so that they could see all aspects of preparation. They needed to be responsible for gear and to know that 'going hunting' doesn't just involve jumping in the truck and letting daddy drive them there. If I wanted them to be strong, independent individuals, I had to stop doing everything for them.

Once I figured this out and relinquished control, I felt like we had reached the next level. I was very surprised how eager my daughters were to break free from the client role and get involved. I was no longer taking my daughters shooting or hunting, we were a family group headed to the outdoors. The night before a hunt, I would tell them to get their hunting gear ready and to be dressed and prepared to leave at a certain time. When we arrived at the hunting grounds, I would hand out gear at the back of the truck. Each kid was outfitted with their unloaded firearm, a set of shooting sticks and a chair or sitting cushion, depending on our activity. They would carry their gear in, and they would carry their gear out. I no longer carried everything for them.

Almost instantly I began to see a change in Alyssa and Jessica. They seemed to appreciate the extra responsibility and developed more confidence, and they each began to develop their own individuality. Each had their favorite firearm and set of gear, and would always voice their preference. Before they graduated from tagalongs, I would hand them their gear. Once they became active participants, they would tell me which they preferred.

By the time they graduated to big game hunting, they were both carrying their own rifles, packs and sticks. During Jessica's first big game hunt, I took her out chasing wild pig out here in California.

We spent the entire day hiking the hills looking for game and she carried all her own gear. When I killed a large boar about midday, she helped me field dress and quarter out the pig. She even packed the back straps and head out of the steep canyon.

My point is, at some point you need to let them start doing stuff on their own no matter what the activity. Hunting allows them to see the different stages of planning, preparation and execution. When they get out in the field, and see the results of all the preparation, they will appreciate all you as a parent have done to get them to that point.

Praise and using yourself as an example

One of the greatest gifts we can give our children is self confidence. From the day they understand the tone and the meaning of encouraging words, they began to develop self esteem. If you think about it, as youngsters, they strive to do well and make their parents proud. When you let them know that they've done well at any activity, it will definitely boost their self esteem and they will continue to improve.

Even before my daughters began shooting, I was making sure that my wife and I were well into building up their self confidence. I began to realize very early on during the outdoor training process that praise was going to be essential during their progression.

Since there are levels of transition in target shooting, like moving up in caliber or increasing target distance, letting your kids know when they've done well will go a long way in helping them achieve their goals of getting better. I made sure that I piled on the praise whenever my daughters did well. Give them praise as often as possible and you'll start to see them becoming prouder and more self assured in all the things they attempt.

When you first introduce kids to just about any new activity, there will be periods of frustration for them as they learn the specifics. In my opinion, if you don't handle these episodes correctly, their interest may wane. Kids have short attentions spans and tend to overreact to small failures. It's important to assist them in getting through these episodes, be it a missed target, a reluctance to move up in caliber or just a bad day.

When the girls stumbled a bit, I would often use myself as an example to demonstrate where exactly they measured up. I would tell them that despite their struggles, they were far better at the activity than I was at their age. As a father, I understand that my daughters look up to me. When they'd get frustrated, I'd often let them know that they were further along in the training than I was at the same age. I noticed with the mention of this and some encouragement, their frustrations didn't last long. I was very careful not to overuse this strategy, but when I did, it was useful in getting my daughters through the rough periods.

Kids also tend to get better quickly if they stick with anything new for long. Once they got the hang of aiming and feeling comfortable, both girls were shooting well and hitting targets out at greater distances. If they started to doubt themselves during the process, I'd remind them how much better they've gotten since they started.

Everyone enjoys being praised. It really doesn't matter what the activity, feeling proud about your participation and accomplishments increases confidence and provides motivation for young and old. It probably goes without saying, but when you see something your child does that deserves praise, even a little, let them know. I can still remember my dad telling me he was proud of me for something I did when I was about eight years old. I don't remember what I did, but I do remember he was proud, and that's all that matters.

Just take them hunting with you

The delay in interest between Alyssa and Jessica actually helped me introduce my daughters to hunting in two slightly different ways. After the first few shooting trips with Alyssa, she began to show an interest in hunting with me. She was far too young to go through the California hunter's safety course, but since the interest was there, I decided to take her out hunting with me as an observer.

Usually after a short target session, we'd clean up the area, pack up and go on a short hike looking for rabbits. I always kept the hunts very short and interactive. I'd ask her frequently if she spotted anything and make sure she saw any game I was about to shoot. Almost without fail, she would ask to carry whatever we got back to the truck. Those short hunting trips started when she was eight years old.

One of my most memorable hunts with Alyssa came when we decided to try some predator calling. She was nine years old and she had already been on a handful of blank stands with me on previous hunts. She had seen predator calling on television and she wanted more than anything to see a coyote running in towards us.

We hiked into this shallow canyon and got set up. I set up her small folding chair and I tucked it into a bush at the edge of the ridge. With her wearing one of my over-sized camo sweatshirts and a camo beanie, she sat down and instantly became part of the terrain. I flipped on the electronic ear muffs and placed them on her head. She pulled her face mask over her tiny face and gave me the thumbs up.

I set myself up a bit in front of her and got ready. Before I started calling, I pointed up the canyon and told her that if we called something in, it would probably come from that direction.

After the second series of calling, a coyote came running out of a thick stand of Joshua trees at the bottom of the canyon. I heard Alyssa gasp as she spotted him. At about 120-yards I barked the coyote to a stop and shot him in an open area of the drainage. I turned around and Alyssa's eyes were huge and she was beyond excited. She had seen the entire stand play out from her chair and we wasted no time in hiking to the downed coyote.

Alyssa knelt down next to the animal and smoothed down the fur. She had seen dead coyotes before, but this was the first trip where she got to see one come to the call. It had definitely made an impression. She quickly got up, grabbed the back legs and decided she was carrying it back to the truck. The coyote weighed about half of what she weighed and after a bit of a struggle, I grabbed the coyote and took over.

That was a memorable hunt for a few reasons. It was the first time Alyssa got to witness a successful predator hunt with me. Her excitement was refreshing and a joy to watch. It was also the first time that I had tested Alyssa a bit by extending our hike-in range. Prior to this hunt, when she would make stands with me, I'd find a spot relatively close to the truck and we'd hike a distance of no more than 75-yards. On this hunt, we had followed the creek drainage for over 400-yards and I let her carry her own chair. I had hunted this spot before and extending our hike distance was no accident. I wanted to illustrate to Alyssa that hunting takes effort and not all stands were close to the truck and easy.

Kids are sturdy

That successful stand with Alyssa taught me a bit about the stamina of children. I had left this particular stand idle because I knew it required a lengthy hike in and I wasn't sure if Alyssa was up for it. During other coyote hunts or short rabbit hikes, I had always made sure that Alyssa was comfortable and that I didn't push her too hard. I kind of danced that fine line between not wanting to physically push her and hunting the way I normally hunted.

What I discovered is that making that decision for them on how hard to go was not my call to make. I realized that on every single early outing, I was making the call on when to turn around or when to quit. In short, I was deciding for them when they were getting too tired to continue. In my opinion, I was not giving them the chance to test themselves and I was stifling their ability to figure out where their limits were.

After that successful hunt with Alyssa, I was no longer deciding for them when they were tired. I did this in two simple ways. First, right before we'd head out for a hike I would tell each daughter that they needed to let me know when they were too tired to continue. I told them that if they got too tired, they just needed to tell me and we'd head back to the truck or stop and rest.

The second method involved letting them know exactly where we were headed before we even took a step. I'd pull them aside and tell them we'd be hiking to that rock or that tree, giving them landmarks so they knew exactly how far we'd be going. All hunters want to know where and how far they'll be going, and kids are no different.

I believe letting my daughters decide for themselves on when they became fatigued enabled them to push themselves and discover their own limits. I watched them stumble, fall, get up and keep going. I've taught them how to be tough and in those early years when the decision to stop was theirs, they did not throw in the towel and quit once.

Other wildlife events

Early in this process, I was fortunate enough to add a unique experience to Alyssa's outdoor training. Here in California the Department of Fish and Wildlife offers specialized hunting opportunities for youths and new hunters. One of the more popular events is the fall season pheasant hunts.

These hunts are geared towards introducing kids to the exciting world of upland game hunting. To dramatically increase the potential for success and to introduce first-time junior hunters to the thrill of flushing game, pheasants are planted for each hunt in nearby fields. During hunter orientation, volunteers head out to the assigned fields and carefully plant the birds for the young hunters.

Participating in these planted pheasant hunts allow new and junior hunters the opportunity to not only hunt, but to interact with experienced hunters and bird dog handlers in a somewhat controlled hunting environment.

While the birds are being planted, the new hunters attend an orientation given by the event's coordinator. He goes over what he expects during the coordinated hunt and strongly suggests that kids and parents alike follow the safety rules and the code of conduct.

Safety is the number one priority during these events and Department staff makes absolutely sure that all hunters are well versed in proper firearm handling.

Once the birds are in place, kids are paired with passionate bird dog owners and their well-trained dogs. The hunting group is then assigned a specific field to hunt. The volunteers will instruct the young hunters when to shoot and when not to shoot, for the safety of all involved.

This is a great opportunity for first time hunters to witness the dedicated coordination between an experienced trainer and his well trained bird dog. Whistles and one-word commands guide the dog through the field searching for game.

If the young hunters are successful, event volunteers show the group how to clean their birds, illustrating the connection between a hunted animal and the meat they'll eventually consume

A dedicated group of volunteers are involved in every step of this hunting process, and each contributes valuable knowledge and experience to the event. They're patient, motivated and direct in an activity that requires all of these attributes in equal amounts. They understand that safety is the top priority and it's not to be compromised in any way. However, they also realize that well instructed kids need to experience the fun of the hunt as well if they're going to continue on as hunters.

These hunts are usually free to the public and are a great way to get youth and family members involved in the hunting activity. It'll also give you an opportunity to meet some of the nicest and most knowledgeable individuals willing to answer any question you may have regarding upland hunting.

During the fall of 2007, a few weeks after I took Alyssa out on her first shooting trip, we got the opportunity to assist on one of these state sponsored hunts. I was invited to hunt clean-up at the organized pheasant hunt. If junior hunters fail to harvest the planted birds, volunteer hunters can work the field after the hunt to hopefully harvest some of the released pheasant. When I spoke with the hunting coordinator, he suggested that I bring Alyssa down so she could experience the event.

The following weekend, Alyssa and I arrived at the staging area for the pheasant hunt. The junior hunters were just entering the fields and the coordinator said we should hike to an observation hill behind the fields to watch the hunt.

At the hill, we watched the hunters, all dressed in orange, slowly walking the sage fields. A symphony of whistles echoed back to us as the handlers worked their dogs. I explained to Alyssa that the dogs were sniffing the ground looking for the birds. I asked her if she'd like to hunt with me behind one of the bird dogs. She nodded enthusiastically and asked if that's what we were there to do.

A whistle from the field nearest us caught our attention. The dog was stiff and on point. The handler guided the young hunter into position and had him slowly walk forward. The young man took three steps and the pheasant flushed and lifted off straight away. The hunter dropped the bird on the second shot.

In these tight hunting situations, positive reinforcement is just as important as corrective statements. During that first hunt we got to see that not shooting in certain situations was far more important than dropping a bird.

Alyssa and I were watching one group out on the planted fields when she got a lesson in safety. In one of the assigned hunting areas, the bird dog was on point. The handler kicked the brush and a pheasant exploded in a cloud of dust and feathers. Instead of flushing straight away, the bird banked left and started flying back near other hunters. The young man followed the bird with his shotgun and then instantly disengaged when he saw the other hunters. Two accompanying adults and the handler all went over and gave him praise for making a safe choice. The young boy's smile was ear to ear as he received the accolades.

Alyssa understood what had occurred in the field below us, and more importantly why the young hunter had disengaged with the bird. She also knew that staying safe anywhere we hunted with the most important thing.

Once the hunters left the field, we met up with one of the handlers. He was eager to work his dog in a field where he knew birds still remained. I told Alyssa to stay behind me and close. Wanting her to get as much out of the experience as possible, I left my shotgun unloaded and simply walked behind the handler.

After a few minutes, the handler's dog went on point. I moved into position and loaded my shotgun. The handler kicked the bush near the dog and a pheasant exploded from the sage and headed out straight away. My first shot clipped the bird, the second shot dropped it.

We ended up shooting two birds out of the field that day. Alyssa really enjoyed watching the dog work and she was very excited that we were able to bring home some pheasant for dinner.

The following year, the hunt coordinator gave me a call a few weeks before the junior pheasant hunt and wanted to invite me and Alyssa back out. To give Alyssa a different look at the experience, I decided to take her out to assist in planting the birds before the hunt instead.

On the morning of the hunt, we arrived early and received some training on how to handle and prepare the birds for placement in the field. The birds aren't just released in hopes they'll stay within the boundaries of the hunting area. Pheasant are gallinaceous birds, which mean they're similar to chickens. A certain amount of manipulation is required to adequately place the birds into the hunting fields.

Holding a pheasant firmly by the legs, and in an upright position, the head is gently guided and placed under one of the wings. Once the head is pinned, the entire bird is glided through a series of figure eights in the air for about twenty seconds while being held. The pheasant is then placed in cover, resting on the wing holding the head. The disoriented bird will usually sit for awhile under the brush, gathering its bearings.

We spent almost an hour planting birds in the designated fields. Alyssa had a lot of fun hiding the birds in the bushes and learned that holding a live two-pound bird by the feet can be challenging.

When we were finished, we returned to the staging area. The junior hunters were just heading out to hunt and I asked Alyssa if she wanted to stick around to hunt clean up like we had the previous year. She looked up, thought about it for a bit and then shook her head. By this time, Alyssa had been on a couple of hunts with me as an observer. She had seen dove and rabbits hit the dirt in the wild, and she knew the difference between a controlled hunt for brand new hunters and a hunt where the only thing controlled was how well you shot.

I believe that this early experience was valuable for a couple of reasons. It illustrated to Alyssa that there were other young hunters like her interested in continuing the hunting heritage. It also demonstrated a different type of hunting for those new to the activity. Since she had seen both sides and understood the differences, she knew that the controlled hunt was put together to give brand new hunters an opportunity to experience everything from the field, to the dogs, to hopefully planted success. Having hunted with me, I think she realized that she was already beyond this training stage, and wanted to continue our journey on our own.

Animal shot placement

During the first year of target shooting, the targets we used were of the normal variety. Clay pigeons, cans, plastic bottles and paper targets were all standard items I'd set out to hone the girls' skills. During a drive home, one simple question from Alyssa made me realize that I needed to add something a bit more life-like to our target selection.

Alyssa wanted to know the best place to aim on an animal to kill it humanely. I guess I had always thought that we would get to that part of the training when she became a hunter. However, her simple question made me understand that I was missing a great opportunity to introduce her to a hunting scenario while she was still a target shooter.

When we got home, I pulled both Alyssa and Jessica aside and showed them a few magazine articles containing photographs of big game animals and predators. In almost all the photos, the wild animals were pictured broadside. Using a ruler, I drew a cross right behind the shoulder and about half way up the animal. I told both girls that this is the desired shot placement for just about any hunted animal. We leafed through the magazine and anytime we saw a broadside animal, I'd point to the proper spot for bullet placement.

I turned the page and there was a nice photo of coyote sky lined on a ridge, perfectly broadside. I asked the girls where they thought the shot placement should be. They both pointed right behind the shoulder, about halfway up. Even though this discussion was focused on animal shot placement, I decided to expand the lesson to include a conversation on safe and ethical shots.

Both my daughters looked puzzled when I shook my head. I asked them to look at the picture and tell me what was on the other side of the coyote. Neither could answer. I asked them where a bullet would go if it went through the coyote or missed it altogether. Again, neither could answer. Using our target shooting sessions as an example, I explained that every time we set up targets, we make sure we have a backstop, usually a dirt hillside, so we know where our bullets go once they traveled through the target. Since the coyote was standing on a ridge and there was no backstop to stop the bullet, we have no idea where that bullet will go so we don't take the shot. I told them if there is nothing to safely stop the bullet behind any target, we don't take the shot. If we don't know what's behind a target, we don't take the shot. If an animal is sky lined, we don't take the shot. This conversation occurred a few years before Alyssa started hunting, but I planned to reinforce shot placement and safe shot selection during our next target shooting trip.

The following month, Alyssa and I were in the desert getting ready to set out targets. I had brought along a piece of cardboard with a silhouette of a broadside coyote drawn on it. I drew a circle in the area right behind the shoulder. This was the first target Alyssa would shoot at that illustrated where the correct shot placement should be on a hunted animal.

Alyssa spent the afternoon shooting at the cardboard coyote. She practiced hitting the circle and did well. During a break, I decided to move the target a bit further out. I walked out, grabbed the cardboard and started positioning it high in a bush, at least five feet above the ground. The placement was clearly not a safe position for a target. Before I was finished, Alyssa yelled that the target was too high and not safe. My point was made. I moved the target back to where it was and walked back to the truck.

If you think your kids will eventually move from target shooting to hunting, set up some animal targets so they can learn proper shot placement. They can get used to seeing a photograph of an animal in their sights, and practice the right place to put the bullet. I found when I introduced these specialized targets during our shooting sessions, it opened up the door to discuss ethical shots with my daughters. Using photographs, it was quick and easy for me to show the girls proper shot placement and examples of safe and unsafe situations they may encounter later on.

Jessica's turn

Jessica began hunting with me as an observer with very limited experience behind the trigger. She had been on a very short target shooting trip when she was seven and she had quickly decided that she didn't like it. Despite her firm commitment to never go again, I kept asking.

One day after work, I headed out to make a predator stand near my house. Jessica caught me getting ready and, to my surprise, she asked to tag along. She quickly grabbed her camo jacket, jumped in the truck and we headed out. Up until this point, at the age of almost ten, she had never come out to watch me hunt.

We drove out to a good looking area, got set up and I started calling. She was right next to me and I could tell she was excited. She searched the terrain looking for movement and remained quiet and still. About five minutes into the call, we both spotted movement about fifteen feet in front of us. A juvenile bobcat, about the size of a shoe popped out of the bushes below us. Jessica's eye's got huge over her face mask as she excitedly pointed to the cat. It was bobcat season and I did have a tag, but the cat was too small and I decided to let it go. We watched the bobcat walk around a bit before he disappeared back into the brush.

When we were done, she was very excited to talk about the sighting. She wanted to know why I hadn't taken a shot. I explained that the cat was too small and he needed a chance to live and grow. I also explained to her that, in my mind, a successful hunt doesn't always mean we kill something. I told her I was just happy she was there to see the cat with me and that there were only two people in the world that got to experience that encounter; her and I.

To commemorate our first hunt together, we took a great photo in the fading light. After that single stand, I began to see Jessica's interest in the outdoors grow.

Even though they arrived at hunting in slightly different ways, once they both got to experience the hunt with me, it seemed like they both began to enjoy it. I would've been content to continue to take Jessica on hunts with me as an observer if she wanted, but after that first hunt, she made it very clear, she wanted to see more.

Push through issues

When Jessica was seven years old, I took her out for her first target shooting session. At the time, I had simply used the age of my daughters as a gauge on when to take them out shooting. Since I had taken Alyssa out for her first trip when she was seven, I figured once Jessica reached that age, it was her turn. This was before I realized how much importance should be attached to their differing maturity levels rather than their age. In fact, it was this trip that convinced me that age was not the proper measuring stick for participating in the shooting sports with my daughters. Before the end of that first trip, I realized that Jessica wasn't ready to start shooting and that I had taken her out way too soon.

During that trip, we had a couple of issues that ended up making a rather negative impression on her that lasted for quite a while. I had set her up near the back of the truck with the semi-automatic .22. The targets were 25-yards out and she was easily hitting them. We hadn't been shooting for more than five minutes, when she suddenly stopped, tears in her eyes.

As I made the rifle safe, I noticed she was holding her hand. One of the spent shells had ejected from the rifle, bounced off the tailgate and landed right on her hand. It was still hot enough to give her a slight burn. After that, she didn't want anything to do with shooting.

While I did understand her hesitation on getting back on the rifle, I made sure that I didn't just let her succumb to her fears. A few weeks after the mishap, I asked her if she wanted to head out again and give it another try. She declined emphatically and from her very animated response, I knew it was going to be a chore to get her back into target shooting.

After more than six months of asking and getting the same response, I had just about given up. She didn't want anything to do with the semi-automatic .22. She wouldn't talk about it, consider it or participate. She would just voice the same concern over and over; she didn't want to get burned by the shell again. It would be over two years before she decided to give it another try.

In 2012, my tenacity finally paid off. I asked her if she wanted to head out to the desert to do some shooting and she reluctantly agreed. This was a few months after the little bobcat encounter and I could tell that she really wanted to conquer her fears.

We pulled off into one of our shooting spots and I set up some targets. One of the rifles I had brought along was a bolt action, single shot .22. Since it was a bolt action, I figured we could completely avoid the ejection problem. To my surprise, she wanted to get behind the very rifle that had burned her two years earlier.

I set her up with the semi-auto .22 and told her to fire when she was ready. She fired a single shot and stopped. My heart sank. I was sure that she had made up her mind about shooting and that she was done. She flipped on the safety and looked up smiling. "Daddy, look I hit the bulls eye!" I looked through the binoculars and sure enough, she was right. Her first shot in two years had hit dead center on the target.

After that, there was no stopping Jessica. She burned through over 300 rounds on that trip, shooting at targets, cans and anything else within her range. Once she got comfortable, I moved her to a set of shooting sticks and a chair. Even during this first real shooting session, I noticed that Jessica was an amazing shot. She became at ease swinging the sticks and rifle to acquire and hit targets out to 75-yards with the .22. After over two years, she became mature enough to conquer her fears and develop a new sense of accomplishment and self esteem. More importantly, during that trip, she discovered how much fun it was to go shooting.

I think it would've been easy for me to give up on Jessica and stop asking her to go. But from the beginning, I wanted to make sure that if they ever wanted to go with me, I'd take them. On the very next trip out, Jessica asked if she could shoot one of my predator rifles. After that, if there were shooting trips planned, Jessica wanted to be part of them. Her sudden transformation from a scared little girl to a tough little shooter occurred over the course of one or two trips, and was amazing to watch. She even developed the mantra of;

"Hovey Tough". If she can push through any pain or anything uncomfortable, she's tough enough to get it done.

It's important to understand what we may consider a minor issue could be very daunting and very real to a child. The slight burn Jessica had received on her first trip triggered a very real negative emotion in her young mind. The pain was brief, but the mental scar lasted for years. It may take them a little time to get over these small problems, but if you're supportive and patient, they will eventually move on. You may be surprised at the demeanor of your youngster once they've conquered that fear. Overcoming an obstacle at a young age does a great deal for their confidence. They may be ready for just about anything.

Eye dominance issues

I have to confess, being a solid right-eyed shooter, I never even thought about this issue. From the first day I put Alyssa behind the rifle at the age of seven she eased behind the Ruger, looked through the scope with her right eye and started shooting. Dealing with the malady of the right handed shooter seriously never entered my mind.

Both Alyssa and Jessica are right handed individuals. Starting them off shooting young, I believed that they would easily train their eye dominance to match their dominant hand. However, since Jessica's interest in getting outside had lagged behind her sister's by three years, her eye dominance may have already been established by the time she started shooting. I believe the time delay may have made a huge difference.

During the second trip out with Jessica we were getting targets set up when I noticed a problem that had slipped my detection during the first trip. As she loaded the10/22 and got settled behind the rifle, I watched her balance her chin on the rifle stock and look through the rifle scope with her left eye. As my good friend Jose De Orta would say, "She's wonky-eyed!"

Sure enough, the following month, when Jessica attended her hunter's safety course, it was determined that she was a right handed shooter, but left eyed dominant. While not a disastrous situation, as soon as I confirmed her condition, I was determined to train her eye dominance issue from left over to right.

After doing a little investigating in correcting eye dominance, I saw one simple common thread suggested in switching dominance from one eye to the other; just use the other eye. Some suggested using eye patches and doing daily eye exercises, but I decided to just stick with what was simple.

Whenever Jessica came out to shoot with me, I'd watch her line up on the rifle and if she was favoring the left eye to aim, I'd call her on it. Every time she tried to use her left eye, I'd say, "Wrong eye," and make her switch. I didn't just make the suggestion I made sure that every shot she took she aimed with her right eye. I think her youth had a lot to do with making the left to right transition easier.

Within just a few trips, Jessica began to use her right eye to aim more often than her left. By the time she was close to her eleventh birthday, Jessica's eye dominance had solidly shifted from left to right, and we left the problem behind us.

The easiest way to determine eye dominance is to extend both arms out in front of you, making the letter 'L' with your thumb and index finger on each hand. Your left hand should display a regular 'L' and your right hand should display a backwards 'L'. Bring your hands together, touching the index finger and thumb of your left hand to those of your right, forming a finger triangle.

With your arms extended and both eyes open, identify something in the distance and put that object in the center of your finger triangle. Keeping your arms extended, close one eye at a time and see what happens to the object in the center. If you close your left eye and the object remains in the center of the triangle, you are right eyed dominant. If you close your right eye and the object remains in the center of the triangle, you are left eyed dominant.

You can further verify this by keeping both eyes open and slowly bringing your finger triangle back to your face. If you keep the object in the center of your triangle, it will migrate to your dominant eye.

Shotguns for youngsters

After a few years of target shooting with the smaller rifle calibers like the .22, .204 and 22-250, I decided it was time to introduce Alyssa to the shotgun. During a few of the target sessions, I had brought along my Remington 870 shotgun just so she could see me shoot it and get a general idea of how rifles and shotguns differed. She was far too small to safely support and fire the 870, but seeing me shoot it was a great way to introduce her to some specifics of the shotgun like recoil and shot pattern.

I can't remember the first time I fired a shotgun, but I can tell you it wasn't until I was in my mid teens. I was close to adult size by then and I simply picked up a single-shot 20 gauge and started shooting. The recoil didn't bother me a bit and I soon bumped up to a 12 gauge and essentially never looked back. For this reason, I really didn't believe introducing my daughters to the shotgun was going to be an issue. I thought, much like the other larger calibers they had fired so far, they'd fire it a few times, get used to it and move on. Immediately after our first shotgun session, I would understand that my easy shotgun introduction as a youth would not seamlessly transfer to my smaller daughters.

The obvious initial factor for me was to wait until I believed Alyssa was big enough to absorb the intense recoil of the shotgun. Having no experience with introducing young children to the punching recoil of the shotgun, I mistakenly used just her age to determine when she was ready to fire it.

When Alyssa was ten, I bought her a Mossberg, youth, 20 gauge pump shotgun. I owned three full sized 12 gauge shotguns at the time, but they were too heavy and long for Alyssa to support and shoot safely. I chose the Mossberg pump because it was lightweight and had an adjustable stock. The stock adjustment was an attractive feature to me because it allowed the firearm to accommodate Alyssa as she continued to grow. I chose the 20 gauge option believing that the lighter gauge would be less recoil for her to deal with.

Within days of the gun's arrival, Alyssa and I headed out to shoot the brand new Mossberg for the very first time. She was extremely excited to add another caliber to her growing resume, and she was looking forward to trying out her new shotgun.

At our shooting spot, I fitted Alyssa with her eye and hearing protection, and I did the same. I grabbed the Mossberg and decided to shoot it first. I set out a cardboard box as a target, loaded three shells into the firearm, shouldered it and fired the first shot. The recoil punch of the little shotgun totally surprised me. It actually kicked more than my 12 gauge. I cycled and fire the next two rounds, again feeling the strong recoil and wondering if my ten year old could handle it.

Once the shooting started, Alyssa was anxious to take her turn. We briefly discussed a good firing stance, seating the stock solidly against her shoulder and gripping the weapon tightly. After a few adjustments, she raised the barrel towards the target box and fired. The recoil thump completely surprised her and I could see tears welling up in her eyes after the shot. I reached for the shotgun, but she pulled it close and said she wanted to fire the next two rounds. She roughly cycled the second shot and fired that one, followed closely by the third. She then weakly handed me the shotgun, rubbing her shoulder. Despite her eagerness to put another caliber under her belt, Alyssa only fired six shots total during that first trip before handing it back to me, a little battered from the kick. Even though the shooting session was short, I was extremely proud of how well she had handled herself.

I learned a few things during that trip that influenced how I proceeded with the shotgun introduction. I knew as the girls got older and bigger, the recoil would become less of an issue. However, until they got bigger, the recoil punch would become something that they needed to conquer and overcome if they wanted to shoot the shotgun. I realized that the mass of the smaller shotgun did not sufficiently absorb much of the recoil of the shot. I also understood that the size and mass of my daughters was going to be a huge factor that needed to be considered during this process.

A shotgun's overall mass will play heavily into the recoil absorption that is experienced by young shooters. Starting kids off on some of the smaller, youth shotguns is always recommended, but what we discovered, is that smaller shotguns, with lighter mass and shorter barrels, still kick pretty significantly. As we continued to move through the shotgun transition, I would discover that this part of the training would prove to be one of the toughest parts of the entire process.

Alyssa is a tough kid and eager to try anything. However, despite her brave face, the Mossberg youth shotgun had hurt enough for her to take a break from shooting it. To make sure she eventually got used to the recoil of the little shotgun, I would have her shoot it a few times on every trip. Within in a few months of starting on the shotgun, Alyssa eventually moved through the recoil and the following year she was regularly busting clay targets with the little Mossberg.

I briefly considered using lower velocity shotgun rounds to ease them through the recoil process, but decided instead to have them push through with hunting loads. Sometimes you just need to yank off the band aid.

When dealing with larger recoil, kids should use youth-sized single shot or pump shotguns that essentially give the youngster a single shoulder punch. I'd steer clear of semi-auto shotguns as excessive recoil may result in additional involuntary trigger pulls. Using a single shot, break open shotgun, or a pump shotgun, loaded with a single shell is the best way to introduce young shooters to the increased recoil and get them used to that shoulder punch.

I think a huge part of getting kids beyond the shotgun recoil, is mental. I explained to my daughters that once they start shooting it, they won't even notice it. I let them know that once they start breaking clay pigeons or hunting with a shotgun, the recoil goes unnoticed in the excitement of success. Make it less about the recoil and more about them conquering the next hurdle on their way to becoming experienced shooters and hunters. When both girls eventually fired the 20 gauge, I made it a big deal that they had graduated to the next level. Make sure you let them know how proud you are of them. Not for firing a shotgun, but because they conquered a fear and moved passed it. You'll be surprised how quickly they forget about the shoulder punch, once they get over it.

Jessica's shotgun turn

Alyssa muscled through the shotgun recoil. Jessica did not. She was absolutely petrified of the shotgun, and in her words, it made her nervous. Once she began coming out with me again, she shot the Mossberg one time and that was it. The recoil startled her and punched her hard enough to leave a bruise. After that, she wanted nothing to do with the little shotgun.

Understanding the differences between my daughters, and building off my experience with Jessica's initial temperament towards shooting, I decided to stay persistent without being pushy. On trips when it was just the two of us, I'd bring the Mossberg along and ask her exactly once if she wanted to try it again. She would wrinkle her nose and politely shake her head. However, I saw a ray of hope in every decline. I could see it in her eyes that she was disappointed in herself for not conquering the recoil of the shotgun. Jessica's personality and tenacity mirrors my own, and I knew that eventually she would shoulder that Mossberg again and conquer her fears.

I believe the competiveness between my daughters also played a role in their progress during this adventure. I watched on several occasions where they'd push each other to try new things. The signals were subtle, but they were there. Since Alyssa had conquered the shotgun recoil, we'd occasionally make trips out to shoot clay pigeons. I'd load up a few hand throwers and a box of bright orange clay targets so she could practice her wing shooting. It wasn't long before she was regularly breaking targets with the Mossberg.

On one trip, the three of us had planned a Saturday shooting day. Out at one of our spots, we pulled out the shotguns and Alyssa and I took turns throwing and shooting clay pigeons. This was the first time Jessica had witnessed Alyssa shoot at flying targets and when she saw her success, coupled with her enthusiasm, I was hopeful she'd want to join in. She declined on that trip, but I could see that something had changed. She had observed her sister moving forward in the shooting process without her and she didn't necessarily like that.

A few weeks later, I had planned a solo predator hunting trip. I was going to head out early and hunt some areas I hadn't hunted in a while. Those plans were shelved when Jessica asked if she could come along. I remember thinking as I loaded up for the day, that I should probably bring the little Mossberg.

Before we even arrived at our destination, Jessica asked if we could pull off and do some shooting. I don't normally target shoot in the same area I'll be hunting, but having my youngest with me, I was happy to change up the plans.

We found a suitable area and as Jessica grabbed her ear muffs, I set up a few soda cans as targets. I grabbed the .22 rifle Jessica usually used out of the truck and also brought out her shooting sticks. I walked to the front and started to hand her the rifle when she politely refused. "No daddy, I want to shoot the shotgun!"

I was speechless. I walked back to the truck and grabbed the Mossberg and a box of shells. Just like I had done with her sister, I gave Jessica advice on stance, shoulder mounting and grip. I loaded up a shell, refreshed her memory on the action and took a step back. Without apprehension or hesitation, Jessica fired the shot. I watched her small frame jolt back and I seriously expected her to hand me the shotgun signaling that she was done. The broad smile I was greeted with warmed my heart.

Jessica burned through an entire box of shells that morning, gaining confidence with every shot. She not only conquered the recoil, but she started to voice her thoughts on why she had been afraid of it in the first place. I must've mentioned a dozen times how proud I was of her. Not for shooting a shotgun, but for conquering her fears. I told her that life is full of episodes where fear or apprehension are present, and learning to overcome those fears and move beyond them, shows excellent character. While I was thrilled that Jessica had tackled her fears, I always made it a point with both my girls that achieving the next level of anything was something they should be proud of.

On the next outing, Jessica broke her first thrown clay target with the shotgun she had feared for almost a year. I decided to do a little filming during that trip and I set up my camera low and behind the girls so we could see them break the clay pigeons. My absolute favorite clip is of Jessica on the last shot of the day. I tossed a clay target out in front of her. She brought the shotgun up, mounted it perfectly and broke the target with amazing form. She then turned around to the camera, flashed a sly smirk and nodded her head in approval. In that one moment I watched my youngest daughter transform from a timid little girl, to a confident young woman.

Her confidence and toughness seemed to grow with every trip. During the very next shooting session, eager to get back on the shotgun, she rushed the shot and paid for it. Drawing down on a thrown clay pigeon, she punched herself pretty good by putting her face too close to her right hand. The recoil essentially pounded her hand into her face. She put the shotgun down and turned to me, nose red and tears in her eyes. The only difference was she wasn't crying. She looked at me and smiled. I asked her if she was alright. She looked at me and said, "I'm fine daddy, I'm Hovey tough!"

I can attribute Jessica's eventual success at overcoming her fears to one thing; her personality. She possesses several personality traits that I had at her age. She's stubborn, at times easily frustrated and tenacious. There is a fire in her that burns when things get frustrating. As she matured, she learned to control this temper and use it to her advantage. This usually meant waiting until she was comfortable and ready to challenge herself. I always provided the opportunities and never pushed her. She alone, let me know when she was ready to slay her dragons.

With any activity, I think we as parents need to pay attention to how our kids solve problems. If you push them or pressure them to achieve, chances are they'll shut down and resent the friction. This may eventually lead to them abandoning the activity all together. Be patient, be supportive and above all, be proud. If the interest is there, they will eventually come around.

Clay pigeon practice

Once Alyssa and Jessica became comfortable on the shotguns, we started incorporating trap shooting into our target sessions. In fact, once they started spending time shooting at clay pigeons, throwing clays and shotgun shooting essentially took over our target practice. We'd get to our shooting spot, unload a couple of boxes of clay pigeons and some hand throwers and spend the afternoon shooting the thrown targets.

During the early trips, I'd use the plastic hand throwers and toss single targets out over the desert. The girls would take turns tracking the flying disk and attempt to shoot it out of the sky. After they burned through a few boxes of shells, we'd walk out and retrieve any targets that didn't break when they landed. As long as my daughters kept shooting, I kept throwing.

The plastic throwers worked great for tossing a single clay target, but they were really tough for the girls to use. They rely more on a flick of the wrist than anything else and both my daughters just couldn't consistently throw targets with these throwers. That meant that I was the designated thrower, and after working through a box of 120 targets, I started to get tired.

Before the next trip, I picked up a spring thrower that operates with a foot pedal. This worked great, and when coupled with the plastic throwers, it allowed me to throw doubles and the occasional triple. It also let me participate in the shooting when the girls were taking a break. They could easily load up the spring thrower and toss clays so I could get some shooting in as well.

I was really impressed with how quickly my daughters picked up shooting trap. During Alyssa's first trip, she was easily breaking one out of every three targets I tossed. When Jessica started coming along, she was averaging about 20%, but she stuck with it and seemed to really enjoy this type of target practice. I was very relieved with their early success. When I first started trap shooting in my late teens, the only clays I broke, were the ones that hit the ground.

When I first started trap shooting, I had a streak of almost 300 hitless clay targets. Having spent years as a rifle shooter, I was completely unaware of the techniques used for successful trap and wing shooting. When the clay was tossed, without fail, I would close one eye; aim my shotgun like a rifle and fire, never coming close to following through. Needless to say, my success rate was low.

I found a few books on trap shooting and proper wing shooting technique. After reading up on the basics, I realized I had quite a few adjustments to make if I was going to experience even a little success. With practice and persistence, I was finally able to work out the issues and become a proficient trap shooter. I was thankful that my daughters were more adaptable in the beginning than I was.

Initially, my plan was to get the girls used to shooting thrown clay targets so that I could get them ready for dove hunting. Alyssa had been busting clay targets for a year and already had one dove season under her belt. Jessica was just starting, and the plan was to take her on her first dove hunt in September.

When Alyssa and Jessica were just getting started, I noticed that both girls thought that shooting quickly would allow them the best chance of breaking a flying clay target. I also saw that they were shooting where the target was and not where it will be. In short, they were always shooting behind the target, a common issue with new shooters. In my opinion, this was because they were applying their rifle aiming techniques to wing shooting with a shotgun. A technical issue I was all too familiar with.

I had to let them know that the techniques for successful rifle shooting and successful wing shooting were entirely different. Using what I've learned over the years, I explained that instead aiming, you really point a shotgun. I explained to them that the shot coming out of the barrel was like water coming out of a hose, and with a good follow through, you could sort of spray the target area with shot. Placing a cardboard box out at 10, 20 and 30 yards was a great way to demonstrate how the shot pattern opens up the further it gets from the shooter.

When they understood that their odds of breaking a clay pigeon increased when the target distance increased, I also had to explain to them that waiting too long would usually result in a miss. I shared a little trick with them that I use whenever I'm trap shooting or hunting upland game. With both eyes open, I mount the shotgun and start tracking the target. As soon as the shotgun is mounted, and while I'm swinging, I slowly say to myself, I-have-time before I pull the trigger. This calms me, allows the target to enter that perfect window of distance and a larger shot pattern, and I feel gives me a better chance of hitting that target.

Even though this type of target practice lends itself more to quail hunting, simulating flushing birds flying away from you, shooting at flying targets obviously has applications in hunting any upland game, including mourning dove. It introduced my daughters to terms like 'lead' and 'follow through', nomenclature they hadn't heard during their rifle target practice. Once they applied what they've learned during our trap shooting sessions, I saw a big improvement in their wing shooting when we hunted mourning dove.

With swinging barrels and moving targets, I made very sure that safety was the top priority. In the beginning, only one daughter shot at a time. I explained that if a target was thrown and flew into an unsafe area, I'd yell 'NO SHOT,' and they'd disengage. As right handed shooters, I would stand on their right side and a little behind them when I'd toss a target. We designated a shooting area, which was usually five yards from the back of the truck. I made them understand, if they weren't shooting or throwing, they stayed behind and out of the shooting area.

Becoming comfortable breaking clay targets will certainly allow new shooters to get a feel for hunting upland game. Hand throwing clay pigeons straight away is a relatively easy shot to make for kids getting used to firing a shotgun, and will help to build confidence. Trap shooting is also a great way to introduce the differences between rifle shooting and swinging a shotgun.

Make sure you spend some time letting your kids know the subtle and not so subtle technique differences in the two types of shooting. We did experience some frustration during the beginning, but much like anything else, the more they practiced, the better they got.

Dealing with frustration

Both my daughters are extremely competitive, especially when it comes to activities they are both participating in. As with most sisters, the girls' successes and failures were closely measured against those of their sibling. Being older and involved in shooting longer than her sister, Alyssa quickly excelled in all aspects of shooting and ultimately hunting.

One of the areas where this difference in skill and success was obvious was in shooting clay pigeons during our target sessions and subsequently in the early hunts for upland game. Alyssa's early interest transitioned quickly into essentially getting better at the shooting sports sooner. She started shooting and hitting thrown clay targets at the age of eleven and got her first triple with a pump shotgun when she was twelve. Her consistent early practice transitioned over quickly to her hunting success.

Lagging behind Alyssa a few years, Jessica did not have the same amount of practice behind the trigger in the beginning as her older sister. Since Jessica accelerated at rifle shooting from the start, and had practiced frequently, she quickly caught up to her sister in this shooting discipline. However, when it came to hitting thrown clay targets with the shotgun, Jessica was a bit behind the curve. She would practice whenever we headed out to shoot and she did get better, but the experience and success gap between the two girls was very obvious during her first dove hunt in 2014.

Since they were both licensed hunters and had practiced frequently over the last year, I was looking forward to taking them out for the California dove opener in September. This would be Alyssa's second season and Jessica's first.

My daughters have always been a bit competitive and sitting in the same dove blind was no different. As the first day progressed, I realized that I may have made a mistake bringing both my daughters on Jessica's first dove hunt. Alyssa missed her first several shots and then started to connect regularly on birds. Jessica had a more difficult time. She was getting close, but she could not calculate the lead on the rocket-like mourning dove.

It wasn't long before she became frustrated and discouraged. I realized that my desire to have both my girls with me on a hunt had probably taken place too soon. The last straw was watching Jessica miss three successive shots on a passing dove, only to have her sister follow up and drop it. After that, Jessica shutdown and the day became less enjoyable and a bit stressed.

I don't coddle my kids, and while I did understand Jessica's frustration, I refused to let her mood effect the trip. I told her that she should calm down and take a break. I also let her know that hunting for me was about making memories and having fun, not about who killed the most birds. Finally, I let her know if she was going to be a baby about the situation, she could go sit in the car.

After resting a bit, she began shooting again. She didn't hit any birds during that first trip, but she realized that she was going to be the only one feeling sorry for herself if she continued to act the way she was acting.

The difference in shooting experience, and thus the difference in early hunting success was something I had not thought about. I figured that it wouldn't be an issue that one was a little better than the other. Thinking about it now, I realized I was way off. I actually worried that during that early frustration, Jessica would decide that she wasn't good enough to continue trying. In reality, it had the opposite effect and was fairly easy to fix.

Three days after that first hunt, I took Jessica out for another try at dove hunting just the two of us. Instead of having to compete with her older sister for shots, I let her take all the shots at passing birds. I gave her advice on shot distance and lead. She still missed a lot, but I could tell that she wasn't as stressed.

That day we celebrated small victories. I had brought several shotguns on the trip, and she eventually moved from the junior 20 gauge to a 12 gauge. Her third shot out of the 12 gauge resulted in her first bird of the day. She only shot two birds on that trip, and she still became frustrated, but it was short lived and we enjoyed our solo hunt together. I made sure that she knew that with practice comes more success. I also demonstrated that even with my thirty plus years of shooting experience, I still miss as well. Watching my occasional misses really illustrated to her that we all miss.

Taking my daughters separately and discussing Jessica's frustrations in the absence of her sister, was an easy fix. Since they're so competitive, making adjustments was far easier when I spent time with each of them alone. Thankfully, shooting moving targets with the shotgun was the only area where Jessica lagged behind her sister. As they got older and better, we once again started hunting together, all three of us, without the tension.

I don't believe I was extraordinarily hard on Jessica during her first dove hunt. As parents, we aren't just there to praise the good; we should confront the bad as well. I let her have her moment of frustration and let her take a break to think about how she was acting. After that, I gave her some options that allowed her to adjust her attitude or go somewhere else. That gave her a clear picture of where I stood when it came to her feeling sorry for herself when she should be having fun. To be honest, I usually deal with these situations in a consistent way. I think about how my dad would deal with these moods, and I do exactly the same thing.

Purchase items that matter

I've accumulated a fair amount of hunting and outdoor gear over the years. Just like anyone, my gear list changes over time as I find equipment that suits my hunting style and increases my overall success. I would investigate items that I thought I could use and either made them part of my regular hunting routine or tossed them on the re-sell pile. For me, gear simplicity is the key. I wanted to carry a minimal amount of gear that would allow me to be comfortable, shoot well and somehow benefited my hunting experience.

When it came time to start outfitting the girls with gear, I wanted to make sure that they were going to use what I used. I can attribute a great deal of my hunting success to being comfortable using easy-to-use, well made gear and I felt my daughters could benefit from my product reviews. If I needed to purchase gear for them, and I did, I was going to purchase the absolute best I could afford, with some exceptions.

The Cricket single shot .22 rifle was a good first firearm for Alyssa. However, I think if I had it to do all over again, I wouldn't purchase the training rifle. She used it three times and then transitioned to my regulation sized .22. The small pink rifle now sits idle in the gun safe, a little more than an expensive sentimental item. I originally purchased it because of its minimal weight, but since the girls have been using shooting sticks from the very beginning, the firearm's heaviness was never really an issue during our early target sessions.

The Mossberg shotgun is also seldom used now. Both my daughters have since transitioned to full sized shotguns, and the small trainer shotgun sits right next to the Cricket in the safe. However, this piece of gear was well used and certainly assisted both girls in getting used to the shotgun recoil and shooting at moving targets. It was a good purchase and a good trainer shotgun for the purpose.

In almost thirty years of hunting, I've been through my share of different types of shooting sticks. After moving through several types, I have settled on the Stoney Point bipod. They're lightweight, adjustable and are perfect for just about any type of rifle hunting I do. I discovered early on that I didn't want anything that attached to the firearm. For me, it's important to drop the sticks quickly if I need to take an offhand shot. I wanted my daughters to understand that having a reliable rest is best, but if things don't always go as planned, they could easily drop these types of sticks out of the way.

Both Alyssa and Jessica have been using shooting sticks since the very beginning. They quickly became used to steadying the rifle on the sticks for small game, predator and big game hunting. I've taught them to easily move the rifle and sticks as one unit to adjust to moving game. I've noticed that both girls even use them as walking sticks when hiking between hunting spots. They each have their own set, and while they are a little pricey, they are worth it when it comes to building the confidence of a new shooter.

Along with my shooting sticks, I carry around an insulated butt pad for sitting on. When glassing distant canyons or sitting on a predator stand for fifteen minutes on frosty mornings, a padded seat cushion is great for keeping you off the cold ground and keeping you comfortable. I believe when you're comfortable, you shoot better. A seat cushion is light and easy to carry, and will keep new hunters comfortable and warm during the colder parts of the year.

Every single rifle I own has a quality rifle sling attached to it. When I started buying other rifles for my daughters, I made sure I also put sturdy carrying straps on those as well. I showed the girls how I sling a rifle over my shoulder for a short hike. When I anticipate a lengthier hike, I'll cross sling my rifle over my head to keep it from sliding off my shoulder. This last method quickly became the girls' favorite way to carry firearms. It gave them the ability to have both hands free to steady their hikes, and in my opinion, was an easier way for them to carry the weight of the rifles without worrying about it constantly sliding off their shoulders.

A quality sling, with a padded shoulder pad is a piece of gear every young hunter should have attached their rifle. I would recommend not skimping on cost here. A cheaply made, low quality sling will dig into your child's shoulder, and make carrying their firearm uncomfortable. The extra money you spend in getting one that is padded and adjustable will be well worth it.

The one area where I was able to save a bit of money in the beginning was on the purchase of hunting clothes for my daughters. In the beginning, I considered them more outdoors clothes, since all we were really doing was spending time outside shooting. When they were younger and still growing, we opted for off the rack camo pants and shirts. When warmer clothes were required, they relied on my hand-me-down hunting sweatshirts and jackets. Since the activities were limited, the cheaper, less expensive outfits were just fine for this early part of the training.

Alyssa wore the less expensive clothing during her early hunting trips with me. Once Jessica started coming along as well, and they both became interested in hunting, I felt like it was time to move them to the next level of clothing specifically designed for the outdoors.

As they got a bit older, and their growth spurts slowed, I decided to outfit them with true hunting clothes made for young women. The SHE brand of outdoor clothing was something they had seen other female hunters wearing on outdoor shows and they immediately gravitated to the brand. The clothing is well made, tough and designed to fit women. Once the girls tried on the gear made especially for female hunters, they were sold.

When they were young, I didn't want to continually purchase the more expensive name brand hunting clothing and have them quickly outgrow it. Their early outdoor clothing came straight from Walmart. It was inexpensive and served the purpose. When their interests grew, I wanted to make sure they wore a quality brand that served them well in the field.

When it came time to buy outdoor footwear for my daughters, I followed the same thought process I had gone through with the clothing. I didn't spend a great deal of money on their first set of boots. I knew that growing kids would quickly outgrow their shoes and I seriously felt it would be a waste of money. For the first few years, their outdoor boots were inexpensive hiking boots. They were functional, better than tennis shoes and didn't break the bank.

When the shooting trips turned into short hunting hikes, the girls started to voice their displeasure with their footwear. The boots were mid-ankle hiking shoes that offered little in the way of protection from burrs and foxtails, and essentially left their socks and ankles at the mercy of whatever we were hiking through. I knew when they started complaining about how uncomfortable their boots were it was time to invest in better hunting boots.

The types and brands of quality hunting footwear are diverse. I won't get into choosing one brand over another, as I believe that's a personal choice. I will however mention that it's important for the boot to fit well, be comfortable and sturdy. Boots should be purchased well before a planned trip or hunting season so your child has time to break them in. I had the girls wear their new boots whenever they could and whenever it didn't interfere with their developing individual fashion sense. You don't want to send your youngster out in a rugged hunting scenario without breaking them in first. There is nothing worse than uncomfortable footwear on a hunting trip, especially for children.

All hunting gear is a personal choice. Some individuals gravitate towards certain brands and are loyal to that particular gear. Whatever your preference, take the time to purchase gear that your young hunters will continue to use throughout their hunting career. If you've gotten used to a piece of gear that you believe increases your hunting success, or simply makes your time in the field more comfortable and enjoyable, guide your youngster to use the same thing. Your product review and experience is far more valuable than a colorful ad or the endorsement of some hunting celebrity that you've never met.

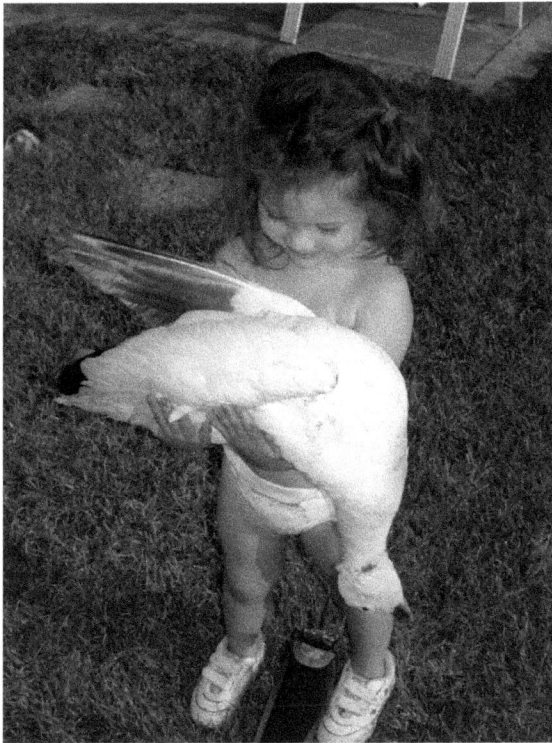

Alyssa helping with a snow goose. She was always the first to meet me when I returned home from a hunt (Hovey 2002).

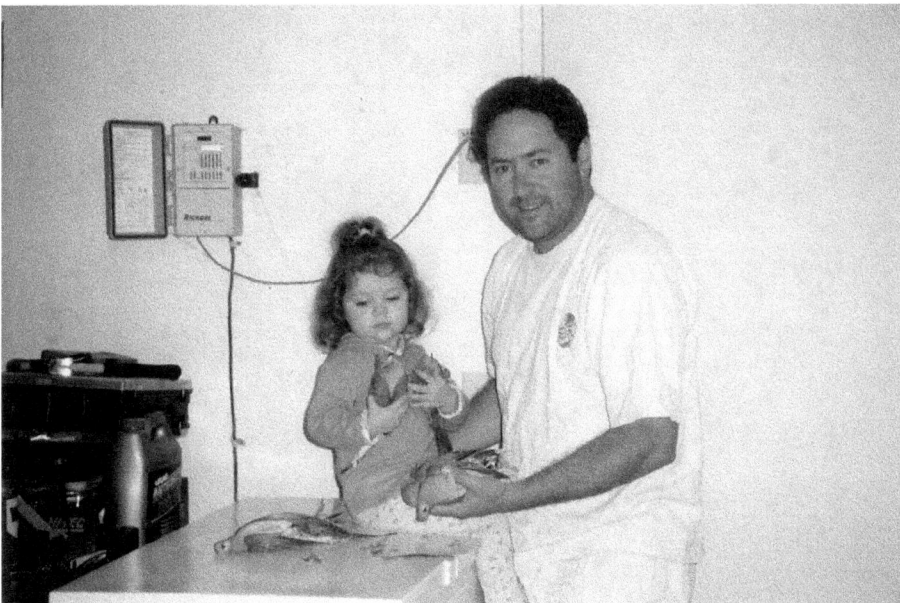

Alyssa assisting me with 'birdie meat.' It was about this age where I saw her outdoor interest blossom (Hovey 2002).

Jessica helping with a bobcat just about as big as she is, about a month after discovering that wild animals are wild and not pets (Hovey 2008).

Our first trip out together. Alyssa would convince me that first year that there was no need for unnecessary worrying (Hovey 2007).

Alyssa shooting her pink Cricket rifle during a trip to the desert. Both Alyssa and Jessica have been shooting off sticks since the beginning (Hovey 2008).

Once Jessica overcame her fears, she demonstrated amazing marksmanship. One of her favorite things to do was to shoot clay pigeons with the .22 (Hovey 2012).

Me and Alyssa during our first successful predator hunt. After this hunt, all she wanted to do was hunt predators (Hovey 2010).

Me and Alyssa after a successful state run pheasant hunt. She was able to watch the well-trained dogs work the fields and the pheasants flush (Hovey 2007).

The following year, Alyssa assisted in the planting of the birds for the controlled pheasant hunts. She found this part of the event more rewarding than the hunt itself (Hovey 2008).

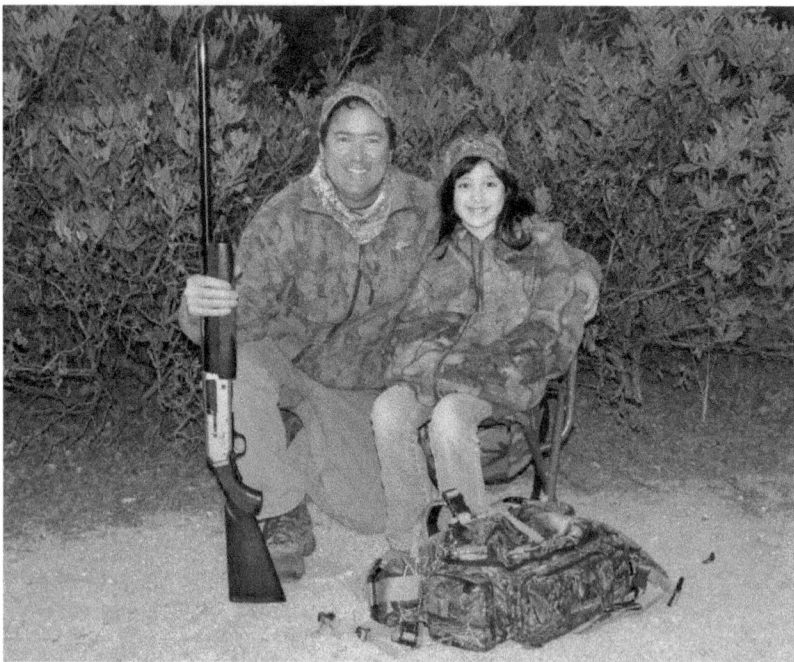

Those smiles say it all. The first time Jessica ever hunted with me. From this day on, Jessica decided that she wanted to be part of our hunting tradition (Hovey 2012).

Jessica showing off her first target. After a slow start, Jessica began participating in our outdoor adventures at around the age of ten (Hovey 2012).

Once Alyssa got a little bigger and stronger, the recoil of the little Mossberg went unnoticed. By her second season she was breaking clay targets with the 20-gauge (Hovey 2013).

Jessica's toughness and stubbornness pushed her through the Mossberg recoil. After an apprehensive start, she conquered her fears and has since never looked back (Hovey 2014).

Shooting clay pigeons quickly became the girls' favorite type of target practice (Hovey 2014).

Within a few trips, both Alyssa and Jessica started to sharpen their wing shooting skills. Their practice definitely showed during the following mourning dove season (Hovey 2014).

Once the girls conquered the shotgun recoil, they both became proficient wing shooters. Here's the Hovey's after a day of shooting clays (Hovey 2014).

Jessica with her first mourning dove as a licensed hunter. Three days after the opener, I decided to take her out alone so that she could hunt without competition (Hovey 2014).

Eventually we moved beyond the sibling friction to hunt together as a family (Hovey 2014).

Quick target acquisition

As we all know target practice and getting used to your firearms is beneficial to being successful in any hunting scenario. The more you use and become comfortable with the tools of the hunt, the more success you'll have. I've always tried to instill this mindset into my daughters as they moved through the shooting process. Once they got used to hitting distant targets off their shooting sticks, I started introducing some techniques that would increase their hunting success in real hunting situations.

One thing that I believe increases hunting success tremendously out in the field is acquiring your target quickly. I've seen some very good target shooters come up short when it comes to real hunting situations. The most common issue for new hunters is getting on the animal quickly. When pursued, wild animals rarely stand still long, and even if they do, getting a sight picture in the scope before they disappear can be something that frustrates hunters that haven't practiced this real life hunting application.

When both my daughters started becoming comfortable behind the rifle, I'd challenge them with some target exercises. At first, I'd tell them to move their rifle and sticks to get on targets to the left or the right of their position. This made them acquire targets that weren't placed directly in front of them. I had them do this quickly but safely. I wanted them to get used to finding targets in different areas within their shooting lane.

Initially, they'd peer through the scope to find the side target. I'd watch them move their heads behind the rifle in an attempt to locate the new target, taking longer than they should. No matter how big or visible the target was, in the beginning, they had a tough time adjusting to this new exercise. Admittedly, I wanted them to get frustrated.

After a few trips, I started giving them some tips that I use to quickly acquire a target. I explained to them that most of the time, I keep both of my eyes open when I aim through a scope. This allows me to raise the rifle, look through the scope and track to the target instantly. It takes a little practice but having both eyes open while you aim will give you a better perspective and more location data for your brain. The more data you have, the quicker you can locate your target.

We spent an afternoon practicing this technique and within a few trips, I started to notice that both girls were finding their targets quicker. To further refine their target acquisition, we would practice this exercise every time we were out.

Another tip I've used for a long time is to identify a landmark near the target I'm trying to acquire quickly. I'll pick out a tree, a bush or a rock adjacent to my target, thus quickly finding my aim point in association with my landmark. Identifying a larger item to track to is incredibly helpful in locating a hard to see target. As a predator hunter, I often use the landmark technique, in conjunction with keeping both eyes open to quickly find a nervous coyote or a moving target in the scope.

Within a year of teaching my daughters these techniques, I saw a noticeable difference in their ability to acquire targets quickly. In fact, I attribute their early predator hunting success to being able to find nervous animals in the scope before the coyote or bobcat had a chance to leave. I believe that introducing them to these easy aiming tips increased their success and gave them the tools to capitalize on their early encounters, no matter how brief.

Offhand shooting

If you think about it, no matter what type of game you pursue, whether its small game, predators or big game, situations will present themselves that will require you take an offhand shot. In my opinion, the most important part of this shooting application is feeling comfortable shouldering the firearm, getting a sight picture and executing the shot smoothly. The best way to feel comfortable shooting without a stabilizing device, like a set of sticks or a bench, is to practice.

Once Alyssa and Jessica got comfortable hitting targets off shooting sticks, to end the shooting session, I had them practice quick target acquisition and offhand rifle shooting. One at a time, I had them stand with their firearm in a safe position. I would identify a larger target out at about 75-yards and tell them when they were ready, to mount the rifle, acquire the target offhand and fire as quickly as they could.

They found their first few attempts at this frustrating. One of the issues for kids that are used to shooting off a bench or a set of sticks is supporting the weight of the firearm when shooting offhand. Being used to shooting off the sticks, the girls quickly discovered that holding the full weight of the firearm steady enough for a shot was a bit challenging. However, after a few attempts, they began to get better and started easily hitting the target. This offhand shooting exercise got both girls familiar with the true weight of their rifles and made field shooting during actual hunting situations a lot easier. After a few trips, this exercise became one of their favorite parts of our shooting sessions.

Having Alyssa and Jessica practice offhand shooting early in the process also taught them to acquire a solid and repeatable cheek mount on their rifle. I believe it's important for any shooter to be comfortable and used to mounting a firearm in preparation for firing. Without a set of shooting sticks to rest on, they began to get used to supporting the rifle weight, consistently mounting it and executing the shot smoothly. I explained to them that I use shooting sticks when I can, but when I needed to take a quick offhand shot, practicing without the sticks was a great way to prepare. As with any training, the more they practice, the better they'll get.

Muzzle management

It's very important to instill proper muzzle management and safe firearm handling to your kids when you teach them to shoot. I believe proper muzzle management is a two-way street. While it's mainly the responsibility of the shooter to make sure that their muzzle is pointed in a safe direction, muzzle safety is the responsibility of everyone in the group. If you or your kids see something unsafe while shooting, no matter who the offender is, they need to speak up and say something.

From the very first trip, I've taught my daughters to not only be aware of their muzzle direction when they're shooting or handling a firearm, but to be aware of other's as well. When they weren't shooting, I wanted them to be focused on the shooter and muzzle safety the entire time we were out.

As the girls transitioned to hunting with me, we established a shorthand signal to continue our safe muzzle practice. During predator hunts, the girls would frequently be lined up right next to me, their rifles firmly resting on their shooting sticks. When the stand was over and we needed to move on, I'd nod to the girls and they would safely unload their firearms as they rested on the sticks. Once that was done, I'd hold my arm out at a steep angle like I was going to karate chop something. The girls have learned that this signal means their muzzles need to be pointed in a safe direction. It's become our personal safety signal and we use it frequently when we're out in the field.

The great thing about our method is that it can be used over distances without saying a word. Last year we were out dove hunting and all sitting together. I went out to retrieve a downed bird and before I left our blind, I made the muzzle signal to both girls. They instantly lifted their shotguns and unloaded them so I could safely head to the field to collect the bird. It took a bit to locate the dove and when I started making my way back to the girls, I noticed that their barrels could be adjusted a bit. I whistled to my daughters and held up my arm, instantly the barrels of their shotguns were adjusted to a safer position without saying a word.

The observation of firearm safety doesn't have an expiration date. Not only do I constantly remind my daughters about safety, they even remind me at times. Practice it early and often, and your kids will not only remember it, but they'll practice it as well.

In early 2015 I took Jessica on a wild pig hunt on a ranch I had access to. We were hunting with another father-daughter pair that we had just met earlier that day. After a few creek pushes and steep canyon hikes, we had two pigs on the ground. After I took care of the meat, we cleaned up and parted ways with the new hunters. On the drive home, Jessica asked me if I had ever hunted with the guy before. I told her that I had just met him and that I hadn't. She thought for a second and then spoke. "That guy is not very safe," she said. She continued to explain that several times during the day she watched him be unsafe with his firearm. I noticed it once and told him to watch his barrel, but she had also caught him a few times. I told her I was proud of her for telling me and even prouder that she stayed focus on safety during the day.

When rifles are resting on a set of shooting sticks, muzzle control is easy to observe and maintain. However, when rifles are being transported to and from the field, making sure everyone is safe is my top priority. Using a rifle sling is a safe and convenient way to carry your rifle when out in the field. However, this convenience can introduce some muzzle safety issues for both new and experienced shooters.

I've seen many longtime hunters completely forget about muzzle management when they have a firearm slung on their back. They bend to pick something up and the muzzle goes from a safe position to being leveled in the direction the person is leaning. Since the firearm is stored on or across their back, all hunters need to be reminded of where that muzzle is pointed when they bend over to pick something up, or bend down to examine a downed animal.

I've taught both my daughters that if they have a rifle slung on their shoulder and needed to retrieve something on the ground, they should face in a safe direction before they bend down. I've also emphasized that if possible they should try and squat down instead. This method keeps the barrel pointed in a safer direction than if they just bent over. Since they've already moved to face a safe direction, their muzzle awareness should become second nature and they should remember to practice safe firearm handling every time they have a rifle slung on their backs.

Handgun safety using the Diamond stance

At the start of our third shooting season, I began teaching both my daughters proper handgun safety. I always have a sidearm with me when I head to the desert, but during those early trips the girls weren't allowed to shoot them. Most young kid's hands are too small to properly hold and control the average pistol. Handguns obviously have shorter barrels than rifles and are far harder to control when it comes to recoil and muzzle direction. For this reason, I did not let my daughters practice with handguns until they were older and bigger.

I can't emphasize enough how much safety preparation went in to introducing my daughters to handguns. I am by no means a firearms expert, but I do know how to be safe and I knew I could safely instruct my daughters on the enjoyment of shooting pistols.

In the beginning, I had them hold an empty handgun so that we could practice a proper grip and shooter's stance. I explained to them that all firearms safety was important, but that more shooting accidents occur with handguns. I didn't want to scare them, but I wanted them to understand that they were now graduating to a more experienced level of shooting.

I explained the mechanics of both a semi automatic pistol and a double action revolver. I showed them how the slide of my .22 semi-auto pistol is propelled back over their hands to load another shell after the shot. This was done in support of a proper handgun grip so they would understand where to place their hands safely on the handgun.

I demonstrated the stance that I wanted them to start and end with while they fired the pistols. I taught them to have their non-dominant leg (left for both girls) slightly in front of their right leg, and their feet about shoulder width apart. Using their arms like the hands of a clock, I told them that their target was straight in front of them at the 3 o'clock position. The pistol, always held with both hands in a strong, proper grip, was to be pointed at 4 o'clock or slightly downward before and after firing. Their trigger finger should be positioned straight and off the trigger until they are ready to engage the target. I explained that the only time their finger should be on the trigger is at the 3 o'clock position. Before and after shooting, at the 4 o'clock position, their trigger finger needs to be straight and off the trigger.

They're arms should be slightly bent at the elbows in what is known as the Diamond Technique for pistol shooting. This allows their arms to work as shock absorbers, dissipating the recoil of the shot. Their upper frame, shoulders, arms, hands and pistol, should be rigid and move as one unit.

I told them that before they fire, they need to announce their intentions to shoot. When they were ready to engage the target, they raised the pistol to the 3 o'clock position, flip off the safety and began firing. When they were finished, or if they encountered a problem with the pistol, they know to reengage the safety, return to the starting stance, with the pistol again pointing to the 4 o'clock position, finger off the trigger.

When the girls are shooting the pistols, I stay close and watch their every move. In the beginning, I would stand almost right next to them to correct their stance or just to make sure they stayed safe. Once they were finished or the gun was empty, I would take it from them, check the action, drop the clip or open the chamber and place it safely back in its case until they were ready to shoot again.

When it comes to handguns, it's best to be overly cautious and pay close attention to kids when they begin shooting them. Keep your kid's size in mind when introducing them to handguns. Start with small calibers and stay there until your kids are strong enough to move up. Emphasize safety, but make sure to let them know once they become aware and proficient, target shooting with handguns is a lot of fun.

These steps are how I taught my daughters how to safely use handguns. Your methods or techniques may differ, but the one common thread should be safety. You should stay engaged as they move through the process and stay close by to assist them. Once they become familiar with safely shooting handguns, it'll just become another fun part of their shooting experience.

Turning your back (proper field loading)

Here in California, it takes quite a bit of driving to go shooting or hunting. Subsequently, once we're out in the field, most of our activities start and end at the back of the truck. Since the firearms are usually handed out here, I decided to implement a fairly easy and routine safety step right there at the tailgate.

On every trip, without fail, I have pushed muzzle management. It didn't matter if the rifle was slung, being held or set up on sticks ready to hunt, I made sure both my daughters were aware of the barrel direction of any firearm within our group at all times. Again, if you continue to mention it, this aspect of gun safety will become second nature.

When the kids were just holding the firearms, this was fairly easy to accomplish. I wanted them to continue this awareness when it came time to load their firearms. I decided to teach them exactly what I do.

No matter where I'm hunting, or who I'm hunting with I load and unload my weapon the same exact way each time. Grabbing the rifle or shotgun, barrel up, I take a few steps away from the group and turn my back, facing myself and the firearm in the opposite direction. I then load the weapon without putting a round in the chamber. I then click on the safety and, keeping the barrel in a safe direction, turn back to the group. The gun is now loaded, there is no round in the chamber and the safety is on. All this is done facing away from the group. Unloading the firearm is done in the same way; facing away from everyone else, barrel facing in a safe direction.

As the girls got older, I taught them this method of loading when we were out hunting. Unloading was done immediately after we were done with our hunting and headed back to the truck. When we returned to the truck and were ready to stow the firearms again, the girls would approach one at a time, handing me the weapon with the action open so that I could see that the chamber was clear and the gun unloaded. I'd stow the firearms and we'd head off to the next spot.

Pass on your ethics

Alyssa and Jessica understand the reason behind seasons and limits. They know what sustainable yield means and why we only take what the resource can handle. They understand why we don't pressure or pursue animals during the time they're breeding or caring for their young. As hunters, these types of talking points can assist young sportsmen in realizing how these aspects of wildlife management all fit together. To form a strong foundation, explain to them that sound science, combined with specific species life history aspects, like the breeding season, produce almost all of the resource regulations in our country.

Ethics is defined by the moral principles that govern a person's behavior. Sometimes I think some hunters may confuse ethics with wildlife regulations. They may believe if they follow the letter of the law, they are demonstrating good hunter ethics. To some extent that's true, but I strongly believe that good hunter ethics is the foundation for successful wildlife regulations.

A great example of ethics being applied was when Jessica and I called in the small bobcat during her first hunt with me. At the time it was bobcat season and I had a bobcat tag, but I elected to pass on the small cat. Stopping there, following the game laws, I could've shot the bobcat. However, my ethics as a hunter made the decision to let it go. Afterwards Jessica was puzzled on why I had passed on the shot. Since that trip was the first time she had been out with me, I thought it was a perfect opportunity to give her a lesson on hunter ethics.

I started by telling her that killing an animal is not the reason I hunt. I explained that I enjoy the outdoors and I love being outside. If I'm lucky enough to take an animal, that's just a bonus. When I brought up ethics, she seemed a little bit confused. She knew what game laws were and the general idea on why we follow them, but I realized she needed an example of hunter ethics.

I told her that every hunter has their own, self-imposed code of rules or ethics that they develop and follow as they mature as hunters. I explained that even though I could've legally killed the bobcat, following my own ethics, I decided to let it go so it could live life and grow. I told her that the regulations allowed me the opportunity to shoot the bobcat, but my ethics, my own beliefs and experiences, decided to just enjoy the encounter and let the bobcat go. She seemed to understand, but I decided to give her another example.

Years ago I was dove hunting with an acquaintance. We were set up on a great flight path and the birds were flying perfectly. After a few downed birds, this acquaintance shot a dove that dropped into a single bush out in front of us. Since he knew where it was, he kept shooting. As the flight slowed a bit, he went out to look for the bird, but didn't spend more then 30-seconds searching. He returned without the bird and decided to keep shooting. When he approached his limit, I reminded him that he still had a bird out there in the bush. He stated that he couldn't find it and that he'd just shoot another one. I walked out and found the bird in less than a minute and added it to his pile. After that hunt, I decided that I wouldn't be hunting with him again.

I told this story to Jessica and asked her if she understood why what the hunter did demonstrated questionable ethics. She knew that he had already shot his limit and just because he failed to locate the downed dove, he should've probably ended his hunt. I stated that in my opinion, he demonstrated weak ethics by not spending more time searching for the dead bird, or at least adding it to his limit despite not recovering it. I also explained that at times, during upland game hunting, birds are lost but the hunter is obliged to spend time searching for that bird.

I continued the lesson by explaining to Jessica that ethics is really a personal compass for how each person should behave in situations where no one is watching. I also explained that doing the right thing is its own reward when it comes to ethics and that it can take many forms.

Over the years, ethics issues of some sort or another have come up while the girls have been out hunting. Last year Alyssa was on a coyote stand with me when a large male came in straight out in front of her at about 120-yards. She got on him quickly and dropped him with a shot to the chest. Within two seconds the coyote got back up and started to leave. I anchored him with a second shot before he took three steps. On the walk out to collect the coyote, I asked Alyssa if she understood why I followed up with a quick second shot. She figured it was so that the coyote didn't get away. I told her she was partially correct, but I also explained that as hunters, we need to make sure that we make clean, ethical shots so that the animals we chase don't suffer. We need to make shooting the animal, the absolute shortest part of the entire hunting experience.

I knew the shot Alyssa had taken on the coyote was well within her range and ethical for her. I believe ethical shots will differ between hunters with different levels of experience. A practiced shooter may feel comfortable with a longer shot, while a weekend hunter may not. Differences in a hunter's experience and preparation will define what each considers an ethical shot. Despite this difference, the main objective of killing the animal quickly and humanely should not change. Just like most hunters, I have a tremendous amount of respect for all the animals I hunt, and I make it a top priority to make sure the kill is quick.

Ethics can also be demonstrated when dealing with other hunters. Last year we got a late start for a mourning dove hunt and when we pulled into our spot, two trucks were already parked right where I wanted to hunt. I was very familiar with the dove flight and they were staked out in the perfect area. As I drove by, I waved and kept driving. I could've pulled in close, but I drove down 150-yards and parked. Alyssa knew the area well and she instantly asked why we were driving beyond our spot. I explained that we needed to respect the other hunters and give them room to hunt. Since they were on the spot first, they got to reap the benefits. She didn't like the answer, but she understood it.

An hour after sunrise, one of the other hunters whistled over to me and motioned us down to the prime flight path. They had limited out and the birds were still flying in their area. Alyssa and I had shot a few birds, but we were definitely at the edge of the good spot. We gathered up our gear and moved over to the hunting area. After we expressed our gratitude, Alyssa and I enjoyed another two hours of really good hunting.

On the ride home she mentioned that it was really nice of the hunters to give us the spot when they were done. I asked her if she thought they would've been so polite if we had set up right on top of them when we first arrived. We both agreed that giving them room was the ethical and polite thing to do. I also explained that I didn't expect them to invite us over. They could've stayed on the spot until the flight ended. Being polite and giving them room ended up benefiting both parties involved.

Another form of ethics is the behavior a hunter demonstrates when they approach a downed animal. I certainly understand the excitement a hunter feels when the hunt is successful, but when I see sportsmen celebrate around the dead body of animal like they've just won the lottery, something inside me cringes. I understand the sudden release of emotion, the instant ease of tension and the realization of a goal achieved, but at a time when one life has been taken, I've taught my daughters to deal with those emotions and show some respect. As my dad once said, act like you've been there before.

I go through quite a few emotions when I approach an animal I've just killed during a hunt. I always feel exhilarated when a hunt is successful, but I also feel a brief bit of sadness at the kill. I think this is completely normal, and this is something I've shared with my daughters. I tell them that this small pang of sadness is a sign of respect and shouldn't be suppressed. I've taught them that being excited at their success is also normal, but at the site of the kill, they need to be respectful. The animal has given its life so that we can eat. That sacrifice is to be honored and admired without high-fives in my opinion.

I am always fascinated when I approach an animal that I've killed during a hunt. I know that no other human has ever put their hands on the creature before me. As a biologist, I always take a few minutes to admire the animal. As I field dress the game, I realize that the very molecules that make up the meat I'm removing from the animal will mix with my own, and I don't take that sacrifice lightly.

In the fall of 2015 I took my daughters on their first out of state deer hunt in the Cody, Wyoming area. After three tough days of hunting, Jessica made an amazing shot on a huge doe. Before we even got up on the animal, she expressed that she was feeling all kinds of emotions after the shot. I sat her down and explained that this was completely normal and to be expected. I told her that the day I stop feeling sadness and exhilaration when a hunt is successful, is the day I stop hunting.

Take the time to explain the ethics of hunting and the flood of emotions that will quickly follow a successful kill with your kids. When they see how you react to certain hunting actions, they will attempt to demonstrate similar actions and they should look to adopt your code of hunting ethics. Make sure you lead a good example so that the next generation of hunters will respect the resource and keep our hunting heritage moving forward in a respectful and humble manner.

Hunter's safety course

All states require that individuals, no matter what age, participate in a hunter's safety course before they can purchase a hunting license and begin hunting. Here in California, there is no minimum age for participating in the course, but many instructors recommend that children be at least ten years old to get the most out of the class.

The state wide program offers plenty of classes to accommodate any schedule, and they're usually offered year-round. The course is about six to eight hours in length and is geared towards introducing individuals that have no hunting or shooting experience, to the activity of hunting. The general premise of the course is to teach students about firearms, firearms use, game laws, species biology and above all, firearms safety. The test presented to all participants at the end of the course focuses on the more important sections of the class. It is not the goal of the instructors to fail anyone that participates in a hunter's safety course. Students are encouraged to discuss some of the material during the breaks, ask questions and to assist each other in understanding certain topics.

For kids, these classes can be intimidating. The participants may be a mix of older kids and adults, and the length of the course may be tough for them to sit through. When Alyssa was ten years old and old enough to take the safety course, my wife Cheryl decided to take the class with her. A few years later, when I signed Jessica up, my friend Jose signed his son up for the same class, and we both attended the day-long course with them.

If you have a young one that needs to take the course, I'd recommend either taking the class with them or at the very least sit in with them as they're trained. Just having you there will put your children at ease, making the learning process easier for your kids.

Most states offer practice tests or booklets online containing all the information covered during a class. Kids or those new to hunting can download information before the class, to better understand the topics covered. I highly recommend taking the time to help your child review this information before they attend the class.

At the end of the class, participants take a multiple choice test to demonstrate their knowledge of the material. The covered information is pretty straightforward, and if you pay attention to the instructor, most find it pretty easy. After the test, the students are given a certificate and a hunter's safety card.

The hunter's safety card is usually a pre-printed cardboard card with your state's emblem on it, the instructor and student's name, and an identification number. When you go to purchase their first license, this information is recorded into your state's data base and illustrates that the owner of the card has completed all the requirements needed to be awarded a hunting license. Once this information is in the database, it will be used to purchase tags, special stamps and future licenses to hunt in your particular state.

Once all the information is recorded, it's easy to see the little cardboard card as nothing more than a keepsake. This could not be further from the truth. In reality, you'll need to place this card with your other important papers. Many states require the presence of this card for non-resident hunters. If you're serious about hunting in other states, you'll want to make sure you don't lose your hunter's safety card.

I don't even remember the year I received my card. I can tell you that I haven't seen the original in over twenty-five years. In 2012 I was headed to Colorado with a bunch of friends to hunt elk. Five days before the trip, I decided to check on Colorado's hunting regulations. I was shocked to see that in order for non-resident hunters to hunt in Colorado, a hunter's safety card from the hunter's home state needed to be provided when the over-the-counter tag was purchased. Luckily, I was able to acquire a copy of my card before the trip, but it wasn't easy. Now, all four of our hunter's safety cards are in the gun safe along with birth certificates and other important papers.

I think if you take the time to review the course material with your kids, the entire process of attending the course and taking the test will be relatively stress free for them. When I went with Jessica, I seriously looked at it as just another part of teaching them how to hunt. I also found it a good refresher course for me.

With a little studying and some encouragement from you, your child should have no issues passing the hunter's safety test. These classes are geared towards educating those with little to no firearms experience, and are fun and informative as well. Make sure they pay attention to all the safety instructions presented in the class, as much of the test deals with proper firearm handling. Taking the course with them or signing up their interested friends will make the entire process fun and stress free.

Shooting with friends

When I first started taking my daughters out target shooting, I was lucky enough to have two good friends that were also interested in introducing their kids into the outdoors. I had hunted with Rito Escamilla and Jose De Orta long before our kids were old enough to accompany us out in the field. Their kids were right around the ages of my daughters and they had all been friends for years. It made perfect sense that occasionally, during outings when I was teaching my girls about the outdoors, my friends' kids could also benefit from the training.

I will admit that adding other kids into the mix took some thought. I wanted to make absolutely sure that everyone stayed safe when we were out, which meant that I may need to address safety concerns of kids that weren't mine. When it was just me and my daughters, I reminded them of gun safety issues constantly. To keep the entire group safe, I felt that extending these subtle and not so subtle reminders to the other kids was acceptable. Before we even started, I struggled with maintaining a safe environment, and not wanting to step on the toes of my good friends. In reality, I felt that hurt feelings were a small price to pay in keeping all our kids safe.

As usual, I had put far more thought into this than was needed. Early on, I simply told both Rito and Jose that if they see anything unsafe that my daughters were doing, they shouldn't hesitate to say something. Without hesitation, they extended the same courtesy to me. From that point on, as the adults, we patrolled all our kids and kept a close eye on gun safety whenever we were out as a group. Occasionally reminders needed to be handed out, but since my good friends and I had discussed how to handle issues before hand, the training of all our kids was seamless and enjoyable.

Like me, Rito and Jose thought that their kids would benefit from training with other kids, and they did. However, beyond the training, the great thing about involving them all on occasion was that they got to share some amazing hunts together.

What I first thought would be a small added hassle in watching everyone, turned out to be a huge advantage. Rito and Jose frequently cited my daughters as examples during shooting sessions, and we all kept an eye on firearm safety.

I've known their kids for a long time and have been deemed their adoptive uncle, a role I accept proudly. Since we've spent so much time in the field with these kids, we all feel comfortable addressing safety issues whenever we encounter them.

In 2015, Jose and I took our kids out for their first big game hunt. We had access to property that held wild pigs and we were both hoping to get the kids on their first big game animals. During the lengthy hikes, the kids started to get a little tired of carrying their firearms. Jose's son, Adrian's weapon of choice was a lever action 30-30 without a sling, a heavy gun even for an adult. During the day, I noticed that since he didn't have a sling, he would adjust the weapon constantly, at times swinging the barrel to get a better grip. Later that evening, I found the specialized gear needed to add a sling to a lever gun and had it sent to Jose's house courtesy of Uncle Tim. Due to my close relationship with the De Ortas, it was never a question of how the gift would be perceived. The ability for Adrian to sling his heavy rifle would improve the overall safety of our group and I knew my good friend, Jose would know that.

I feel very fortunate to have gone through part of this training process with my good friends Rito and Jose. To me, they are closer than brothers. The relationships me and my daughters have built with them and their kids will last a lifetime. As I get older, I start to see my time outside as more of a time to spend with family and friends.

I look at hunting trips as more social than anything else. I used to hunt a great deal by myself, and while I occasional still do, I find it much more rewarding to head out with others that share that same passion.

Initially, when I first thought about increasing the group size during this process, I had some reservations. It certainly took a bit more coordination when we added other kids to the activity. However, looking back, the entire process was well worth it. The camaraderie, the times we've shared in the outdoors, and the first time hunting experiences that all the kids got to experience was an unexpected bonus.

If you plan to teach your kids how to shoot, I would strongly suggest asking your friends or neighbors if they'd like to participate. As long as safety stays the top priority, the rewards for involving others not only add to the experience, but will benefit those that may not know the first thing about getting involved in the shooting sports. Once I began teaching my daughters, I was a bit amazed at how many of their friends wished they could learn to shoot.

Including the kids of my good friends added a social component to the entire process; one I could tell my daughters really enjoyed. In the blossoming camaraderie and the ever advancing skill of all the kids, we developed a group hunting tradition that continues to this day.

I've also noticed that in this group dynamic, successes are more celebrated and small failures glossed over and quickly forgotten. Now, close to a decade after meeting Rito and Jose, they have become consistent members of our hunting group and some of the best friends a person could ask for. My daughters enjoy their company and when hunts are planned, we always contact the Escamilla's and the De Orta's to see if they can go.

Not just shooting and hunting

From the beginning, this journey has been more about spending time in the outdoors with my daughters and less about shooting. I had two self-imposed rules when we first started; have fun no matter what we did, and every time they asked me to go, I'd take them.

As our family outdoor tradition continued to grow, I started to reflect on how I was raised. Frequent camping trips and time outdoors were all part of growing up for me. Times with my dad on those trips are still some of my favorite memories of him. He'd load us into the VW van and head for the back hills for an overnight adventure. Our only requirement during those early outings was to find a flat spot to park the chubby vehicle. We'd explore the historic towns of central and northern California and find places to pan for gold. As a family, we'd build bon fires you could see from the moon and end the evening staring into the glowing embers. Those childhood trips are where my spark of adventure started and I am beyond thankful that my dad opened that door for me.

One of the things I remember about those trips is that my dad was always prepared. He had tools and spare parts packed in the back of the van in case we broke down. A CB radio wired to the dashboard kept us in touch with travel friends or people that could rescue us if needed. He also made sure he never took the bus anywhere he couldn't drive it back out safely. These subtle precautions taught me to prepare for the unexpected when I started heading out on my own. He taught us to respect the wilderness and to take care of ourselves if something went wrong. My dad taught me to adapt to difficult situations, deal with them and then move on.

My daughters knew that before we left the driveway, my truck was loaded with all the emergency gear and provisions in case we ran into trouble. However, I wanted to teach them to be more aware and self sufficient when we were out exploring in the desert. I wanted them to understand that daddy wasn't always going to be there to fix the problem and that sometimes they needed to depend on themselves.

Thanks to a summer of snake runs near the foothills of our home when they were just toddlers, both girls were well versed in snake identification by the time we were making regular trips to the desert. When we did encounter snakes, we'd carefully check them out, and without fail, both Alyssa and Jessica could identify the species. Their early exposure to snakes made them more aware of what may be lurking in the rocky crags of the desert, and it taught them to be careful.

When Alyssa was just nine, I let her sit on my lap and steer my truck around some open spaces in the wild. She enjoyed the control of taking the truck wherever she wanted, and I was a bit surprised that her feet could reach the pedals. While she enjoyed the new driving activity, I had far different motives for letting her take the wheel. Call it cautious or paranoid, but if it was just going to be me and my girls out in the middle of nowhere, they were going to learn to drive long before it was legal to do so.

By the time the girls were ten and eleven, I was letting them drive the truck as I gave careful instructions from the passenger seat. We'd drive the well-graded power line roads so they could get used to how much control they had over the vehicle. I had them do everything from starting the truck, putting it in gear and doing three-point turns to reverse course. I made them practice stopping the vehicle and then accelerating to develop skills they would need in real life applications.

We practiced all the safety things you can do in the wide open spaces of the desert. They became so competent and confident in their abilities behind the wheel that I would toss them the keys and tell them to drive us to the next spot whenever we were out in the desert. They enjoyed this new activity so much, that after the shooting was done they would eagerly ask to go driving.

While my initial reasoning for letting my daughters get behind the wheel was overall safety in case I was unable to drive, our lessons had an unexpected benefit. In my opinion learning to drive can be both an exciting and terrifying time in a young adult's life.

They are at the very edge of independence, and for most, it may be their very first major responsibility they've had to deal with. This can be a lot of pressure for a young adult, especially if they haven't spent a great deal of time behind the wheel. Getting both girls started early has not only given them a great deal of driving experience, it has given them the opportunity to get used to driving long before they take their actual driving test. In a sense, their early training has completely removed the novelty and the pressure of learning how to drive.

My dad not only put me behind the wheel at a young age, but he also made sure that if repairs needed to be made, I was right there next to him, learning what I could. The basic automotive information I carry with me today was learned at the back of that VW bus next to my dad. Once the girls were ready and old enough, I had every intention of passing on that automotive knowledge.

Since you rarely have to deal with emergency auto repairs in your own driveway, I decided to keep tools with me when we were running around the desert. Most of the car repairs I've participated in all came unexpectedly on the side of a road someplace, and at the side of the road is exactly where I began to train my daughters.

During our second year out, Alyssa and I decided to head out for an early season predator hunt. We found a great looking spot to start our day of calling. We got set up and as soon as we started, I spotted a raven dive-bombing to our right. Through the thick brush I spotted a coyote coming in fast about 75-yards out. Unfortunately, he was directly downwind and when he moved behind a bush, I never saw him again.

We grabbed our gear and made the short hike back to the truck. Alyssa noticed the problem first. Coming in on the graded road we had punctured a tire and the right rear was as flat as it could get. We stowed the hunting gear and I decided to turn a slight inconvenience into a teachable moment.

I showed Alyssa where the jack was located and how to drop the spare tire from the rear of the vehicle. Using small sections of wood, I instructed her on how to place the jack under the car. With some help, we loosened the lug nuts. I showed her how to use the jack handle to jack up the truck so she could remove the tire. Helping only when she needed it, Alyssa moved through the challenges of changing a truck tire all by herself.

After we were done, we put all the tools away and got back in the truck. I could tell that Alyssa thought the lesson was over. I was proud of how she had taken control, listened to instruction and muscled through the entire process. Now, back in the truck, she was ready to continue hunting.

We got back to the main road, and instead heading out to the desert, I made a right and headed back into town. Alyssa was puzzled and instantly asked me where we were going. I asked her how many full tires we had. She still looked puzzled. I told her that I never head out anywhere in the outdoors without a full spare tire and we needed to get it repaired before we went anywhere else. She understood, but I could tell she was disappointed that we had to end the day early.

A month later she got a clear illustration of how important being prepared is. Deep in the desert, several miles down a two-track we cut another tread in the same right rear tire. Alyssa jumped out and instantly started grabbing the jack and lug wrench. Within ten minutes we had the tire changed and the tools put away. She wanted to do it all by herself and I let her. Back in the truck, Alyssa knew the day was over as we headed back to town. As we drove I looked over and told her it was a good thing we had gotten the spare fixed from the last trip. This time she got it.

Many of the roads we travel are well worn two-tracks and in relatively good condition. However, every once in a while a dry wash will get sanded in and make crossing it a bit dicey. A few months after Alyssa became well versed in changing tires we were once again out looking for places to hunt. We were exploring a new area and I dropped into a dry drainage to get to the other side. Half way across I felt the back end of the truck shift sideways and start to sink. I could feel that it wasn't anything serious, but I decided to show Alyssa some of the tricks I use when I get the truck stuck.

We jumped out of the truck and I explained the situation to her. I told that if the back tires kept spinning, they would eventually sink in the sand and could bury the axle. I asked her how she thought we should handle it. Building off what she knew about changing tires, I was impressed when she suggested we use the jack. I told her that was a great idea, but we had a few other things we could try first.

I grabbed a shovel from the back of the truck and showed her how digging out the back tires will give the wheels room to roll out. I also explained how letting out some air in the back tires would increase the surface area of the treads, giving us more traction. After a little digging, we jumped back in the truck and I switched the truck to 4 HD drive. I told Alyssa that now instead of two drive wheels, we had four. With relatively little effort, the truck lurched out of the sandy river bottom and we easily reached the hard pack on the other side.

Back on the trail, I told Alyssa that she now understands the basic techniques for getting a vehicle unstuck when the back wheels start spinning. She seemed happy to add to her growing outdoor experience, but I could tell she had a question. She reached over and tapped the 4HD dial and asked why we hadn't used it when we first got stuck. I explained that I usually flip to four-wheel drive when conditions get iffy, but I wanted to teach her something new about being prepared. I was glad that she was listening to what I was teaching her and figuring out different ways to deal with emergency situations on her own.

Along with the standard tire changing and driving strategies, both girls knew exactly where I kept both first aid kits during our outings. Fortunately, we never had to use anything more serious than band aids, but having them in the truck gave us all piece of mind.

All these aspects of preparedness and safety are very important for your youngster to know about, especially if you're taking them places that are somewhat remote. While being able to address unexpected issues in the field is a valuable trait to possess, I always make sure that I don't take any unnecessary chances just because I can get out of certain situations. When I'm out in the field with my daughters I think about being safe and not over extending my abilities. Of all the preparation and safety tips I've taught my daughters, staying within their abilities and understanding their limitations are the most important.

Offseason activities

I found it relatively easy to relate personal attributes gained through participating in other activities, back to the shooting sports. Most of these offseason responsibilities had very little in common with shooting or hunting. However, the personal growth and the natural progression of maturity are very much relatable to increased success in just about any activity. As parents, you start to realize that having your kids participate in anything is so much more about building character and integrity in your child, than about the activity itself.

In 2010, me and my wife, Cheryl decided to enroll Alyssa and Jessica in a new workout craze called CrossFit. Cheryl is a certified CrossFit coach for our local gym and has had the girls involved with this popular and specialized training since they were nine and ten and half. Focusing on the benefits of muscle confusion, CrossFit training involves developing core strength and coordination through a multitude of timed work outs of the day or WODs. Utilizing proper form and conditioning, individuals develop personal records or PRs by pushing themselves in these timed WODs and bettering their time for each event. Despite the gym camaraderie and the team-like atmosphere, growth and personal success is very much individual.

I'll be honest, when we first enrolled Alyssa and Jessica in CrossFit, I saw it as nothing more than an activity that would keep them occupied and entertained during the hunting offseason. Personally, I thought that both girls would eventually tire of the repetitive gym routine and workouts scheduled three times a week. I was wrong. Over five years after their original enrollment, both of my daughters stay active in the workout sport.

My original thoughts that CrossFit was going to be nothing more than a filler activity has completely changed. I now look at the early growth and development my daughters achieved during the strength training and structured workouts as being one of the most beneficial periods in their young lives for personal development. I have watched them get stronger both physically and mentally. I have seen Jessica's early timid and somewhat fearful personality evaporate; replaced now with a young woman that is tough and willing to try anything adventurous. Those fears were conquered in the walls of the Crossfit gym. She has learned to tame the fiery flame of frustration and has turned it into an obedient tool of will. Her physical strength is amazing and her toughness makes me smile. She is and will always be my little firecracker.

Alyssa has become what can only be described as a beast. She has attended the three day a week workouts religiously and has more PR's than she can remember. She has excelled at strength training and instead of boy band posters adorning her walls she decorates her room with the top athletes of CrossFit. She is the gym sweetheart and I have no doubt that she could easily beat me in arm wrestling. I have watched her go from daddy's little girl, to a young woman that can physically take care of herself.

Beyond the physical attributes of their gym training, the one common thread I've seen emerge during their early growth is confidence. I believe a solid foundation of self confidence can be the most important personality trait that any young person can obtain. I feel that self confidence and self esteem go hand in hand, and getting youth involved in any activity that can increase those confidence levels is worth pursuing. In a world where many believe that they should just be handed things in life, achievements through hard work and dedication will increase their self esteem and will guide them to lead rather than follow.

With the exception of each being members of the Girl Scouts from about kindergarten on, neither of my daughters were interested nor participated in any team sports until Alyssa's first year of high school. Building off her years of CrossFit strength training and workout coordination, Alyssa was selected to try out for her high school track team. Stronger than your typical freshman girl, she won a walk-on spot on the shot put and discus squad. After a single tryout of both events, the high school track coach asked her to join the team, and Alyssa excitedly accepted. Within weeks of becoming part of the track team, Alyssa's character was tested.

I was part of a team sport through all four years of high school. I played soccer for the Dos Pueblos Chargers and my time as part of a championship team represent some of my favorite high school memories. Being part of a team taught me responsibility, provided me structure and it demonstrated that with hard work came reward. Having other members of the team depend on my involvement also helped develop my character. I was excited that Alyssa had chosen to become part of a high school team. Unfortunately, only three weeks after becoming part of the track team, she had a serious change of heart.

One thing Alyssa had not taken into consideration before joining the track team was how much time was required during the season. The shot put and discus group practiced 2-3 hours a day, five days a week. This of course kept her from attending her CrossFit training, something she dearly loved.

Three weeks after joining the track team, she came to us in tears, stating that she wanted to quit. She explained that the training was harder than she had originally thought and that the daily after school practices interfered with her free time. We let her vent and present her arguments, most centered on the conflict between track and CrossFit. Once she finished I asked her one simple question. I asked her if she had already committed to her new track coach. She nodded that she had. I told Alyssa that giving her word to be part of the track team is everything and that she had to honor that commitment. This was not the answer she wanted to hear, but I believe it's important for kids to understand that if they make a decision and give their word, they need to see that decision through.

A few weeks later Alyssa participated in her first track event and came in third as a walk on freshman. After that she immersed herself in track.

As parents, I think it would've been easy for us to give in and let Alyssa quit track, but that's not how I was raised. I wanted to teach my girls that character is very important and sticking by your decisions demonstrates good character.

These offseason activities gave the kids the opportunity to develop coordination, strength and confidence. They also introduce them to structured practices, the responsibility of performing and independence; all positive attributes, creating a solid foundation for the challenges of shooting and hunting.

Take the time to take photos

I've been very fortunate that the arrival of my daughters coincided with the arrival of digital photography. From the very beginning, even before they came out with me, I was taking photos of my girls.

Do yourself a favor when you're out with your children, remember to commemorate the time with them outdoors. I have two cameras that I carry with us on every trip. One is a high-resolution digital camera that I carry in a pouch on my belt. If there is a small lull in the action or a situation where I want a photo, the small camera is within easy reach.

I also have a nice SLR digital camera that I use for end-of-the-day shots or timed photos of me and my daughters. No matter the adventure, I make sure that I take plenty of digital photos of the day. They are the real trophies of our time together, and they will be a lasting memory that your family will enjoy for a lifetime.

I've been taking photos of my outdoor adventures from a very early age. I still have an old Polaroid photo of the first trout I ever caught when I was nine. I'd take photos of my fish and game, carefully framed with the gear I used. Since I was usually alone, these early photos never included pictures of me. Once I started hunting with friends, I figured better photos would follow. However, it didn't take me long to learn that none of my friends or family could take a decent photo of me and my trophy. I would anxiously open the developed photos with high hopes only to find out of focus, unframed, absolutely terrible pictures. It was for this reason that I asked for and received a 35 mm camera that had a self timer on it for my seventeenth birthday. Since I now could take photographs on my own, I began to understand how good photos should be taken.

As technology has greatly improved over the years, you would think that taking a bad digital photo would be impossible. Unfortunately, despite this cutting edge technology, I still see very poor quality digital photos. Since this section deals with capturing special photographic moments, I think it's important to cover a few easy tips that will greatly improve the quality of your outdoor adventure photos.

I find that the absolute best natural lighting for photographs is in the early to mid morning, or the mid to late afternoon. In these conditions the lighting is softer and easily managed in photographs. These softer lighting conditions allow for differing photographic techniques. If I am taking digital photos in these conditions, I will always use a flash. Using a flash in ideal, daytime conditions will sharpen your subject's contrast and give you a better photograph.

In ideal lighting conditions, I will typically set up the subject with either their back to the sun or position them so the sun is striking them from the side. I try and stay away from having the subject face the sun to avoid issues with over exposure and shadows from the photographer's position.

The worst natural lighting for photographs in my opinion is when the sun is high in the sky. On a clear day, the lighting conditions from around noon until 2:00 PM can be very bright and difficult to work with. Shadows are harsh during midday and it's difficult to get good lighting for quality photos. When I need to take outdoor digital photographs in these lighting conditions I look for shade. Getting the direct light off the subject will allow you to use the flash to capture more detail and better contrast.

Once I have an animal on the ground, I like to take the time to position the game so it'll look good in a photograph. I'm always respectful of the game and make sure that any wounds or excessive blood is hidden from view. This is just my preference. My goal is to commemorate the hunt so I can remember all the specifics of the day. In my opinion gaping wound channels and excessive blood detract from a good photograph. We all know how the animal got there. We don't need to see the gore.

If possible, I like to position the animal in an area with an uncluttered background. If the vegetation behind the hunter is heavily vegetated, cluttered or dark, you will lose definition and contrast in the photo. I will try and drag the animal to an area with a better background to enhance the subject and make sure the focus is on the hunter and their prize. I like to try and have open sky behind the hunter and take the photo from a low position, highlighting the animal against the lighter background.

For big game, I like to tuck the legs under the animal to make it look like it's in a seated position. This also adds stability to the game, giving you the option to pose it or adjust it if needed. For larger animals, this may not be an option, so I'll arrange the front legs together as well as the back legs. The body of your trophy should be free of burrs or any type of vegetation. Take the time to smooth down the hair and remove any foxtails or burrs. The hide of the animal should look smooth and natural.

Most big game animals will drop their tongue after death. I've seen so many really good looking photographs ruined by the animal's tongue hanging out of its mouth. Make sure that the tongue is either positioned on the back side of the mouth and out of view, or shoved back into the mouth. A quick fix is to simply remove the tongue before the photos, but this may increase the presence of blood in the picture. Whatever your preference, hide that tongue.

Take some time to pull any weeds or grasses that may be in the way of your trophy. Many good photographs are taking from a lower angle and nothing is more irritating than having vegetation in the foreground distracting the viewer. I like to make sure most vegetation is removed from the area immediately in front of the animal's position, and in front of where the camera or photographer will be. Once you're finished, step back and inspect the scene. It's easy to do and will definitely enhance your photos.

Even when I have friends or family members with me, I will set up my tripod, use the self timer on my SLR and take my own photos. I just know that after many years of practice, I can frame and take much better photos on my own.

Using a tripod, I can set up the camera and start to frame the image I want. I will have the subject kneel down behind or next to their trophy and face the camera. Once they're positioned, I can move the tripod forwards or backwards to frame things perfectly. I'll occasionally use the zoom function on the camera to bring the image in and out, but for the most part, I find moving the tripod is easier. If I am also going to be in the photo, I'll set up the hunter just off center so that there will be room for me in the photo.

In most digital cameras, the center aperture is where the camera will pick up the focus. When taking a manual photo, you depress the shutter button half way which activates the focus function. Many digital cameras will give you an indicator that the focus subject has been detected. My camera beeps once and the center aperture turns green. This signifies that the subject in the center of the frame will be the focal point. Completely depressing the shutter button takes the photo. This is how most digital cameras operate.

When you set up for a self timed photo, the focus principles are the same. The only difference is that when you fully depressed the shutter button, the camera delays the taking of the photograph for several seconds. If you don't pre-focus the self timed photo on the subject just like you do when you take a manual photo, the focal point of your timed photo will be behind your subject and the photo will be out of focus.

To keep this from happening, just before I depress the button on a self timed photo, I rotate the camera on the tripod slightly so that the center focus aperture is on my subject and then depress the shutter button half way. This tells the camera where I want the focal plane. I then rotate the camera back to where I want the photograph framed, and then completely depress the shutter button. This little trick allows me to get perfectly focused, well framed digital photos with the self timed SLR just about every time.

Since you have the option of taking many photos, try experimenting with different photo angles. While I do enjoy the standard trophy photo set up where the plane of the animal is perpendicular to the camera, I have come to favor more of an angled shot where the head of the trophy is in the foreground and the body is positioned at an angle to the camera. The hunter can be positioned at the same angle, behind the animal, giving the scene a different and unique perspective. I find that these types of photo arrangements are perfect for a portrait photo orientation. Once you've taken a few of the standard oriented photos, try experimenting with different angled pictures. I think you'll be surprised at the uniqueness of some of your memorable shots.

Probably the best thing about digital photography is that you can take just about as many pictures as you want. I always take as many as time permits. I have outfitted both cameras with high capacity memory cards so I don't have to worry about photo storage. I have a fully-charged spare battery for each camera as well. Most digital cameras have larger viewing screens so you can preview the photos you've just taken, giving you an idea if you've captured the image you're looking for. So don't be afraid to take a bunch. You can always sort out the good photos from the questionable ones once you download them. Keep in mind that once the skinning and butchering of your game starts, your opportunity for taking good photos is pretty much over.

Just about all smart phones nowadays are equipped with digital cameras. Some have incredible resolution, photo editing options and once the photo is stored in the phone, it makes it far easier to share with others through emails, social media and texts. I have friends that don't use standard digital cameras at all when they're out in the field, and rely solely on their smart phones to capture special images. With today's advanced technology, I can certainly see why they do this. However, I haven't reached that point quite yet. I am used to using my digital cameras and am very happy with the results. The size of today's digital cameras and SLR's make it easy to pack during outdoor adventures. Both of mine have an auto shut off feature which conserves the life of the batteries and an enormous amount of photo storage.

Today's smart phones will quickly drain batteries, have limited storage and are certainly not the device of choice on a multi-day trip to capture those special moments. If you want high quality photographs of your adventures with your kids, make sure you pack a digital camera. They are super easy to use, small and relatively inexpensive.

Regardless of what you choose to capture your outdoor memories, make sure you take photos whenever you can. Once the trip is over and the meat is gone, all you'll have is the memories, and hopefully lots of photos to commemorate those adventures.

Unexpected creativity

Throughout this journey, I have been pleasantly surprised at what the girls brought, individually to this process. Thinking straight forwardly, I figured I would guide my daughters through the mechanics of shooting and let them decide if they enjoyed it or not. I knew that their training may eventually lead them to the next level, and hunting with me. What I didn't expect was the different ways in which Alyssa and Jessica would embrace the different aspects of the outdoors.

When the wild game came home, both my daughters were used to helping me with the meat processing. What I started to notice is that Jessica wanted to keep her portion separated from the rest of the meat. From about the age of ten on, my daughter Jessica showed a strong interest in baking. Known as the Angry Baker for her occasional, pan-banging tantrums in the kitchen, she has produced some truly amazing dishes for a young baker. When she became a part of the Hovey harvest team, she saw an opportunity to create some creative dishes out of the animals she herself hunted.

After breasting out her first dove, she pounded out the game meat and prepared it in a delicate roulade. After that, I started to see her wheels of culinary creation turning whenever we'd return after a successful hunt.

Back straps of her first big game animal, a wild pig, were pounded out, breaded and lightly fried. She not only prepared the dish, but presented it with ranch dressing for dipping. The wild pork came out tender and delicious.

A few weeks after the cottontail opener out here in California, Jessica not only shot her first ever rabbit, but she ended up taking her first limit of rabbits. As we cleaned them out in the field, on the tailgate of the truck, Jessica started thinking about recipes for the tender rabbit meat. After searching the internet, she decided to try bacon-wrapped, pan seared rabbit with a special sauce.

What I began to notice was that Jessica seemed to gravitate towards creating unique dishes out of the hunted game. Almost without fail, on the drive home, she would ask me what I thought she should make. I would always suggest that she make the call on what she wanted to create and we were never disappointed.

After a slow start, Jessica found an enjoyable angle where her cooking creativity could shine. No matter what meat we were able to bring home, Jessica turned it into a dish that was visually amazing and beyond delicious.

Trophies of their hunts

Almost from the beginning, I noticed it became very important for both my daughters to memorialize our time outside; more so during the hunts than with the target sessions. For me, remembering my time in the field has always been about taking photographs. It doesn't matter what I'm doing, if I'm in the outdoors, I'm taking pictures. This of course continued when my daughters started joining me. To commemorate some of our more memorable trips, I'd set up the tripod at the end of the day and take a group photo. These photos have become some of my favorite mementoes of my time outdoors with my daughters. While my daughters do have nicely framed pictures hanging in their room from our time outside, they made it clear early on that they wanted additional souvenirs of their successes.

Immediately after a successful hunt, my daughters would start searching the surrounding area for their spent brass. I had mentioned that somewhere in a drawer, I still had the shell of my first big game animal. Wanting a keepsake of their first hunts, they'd make sure they found the casing and carefully bagged and labeled them. Alyssa even went so far as to keep the brass of the very first coyote I called in and shot with her at my side. With a little creativity, I turned that memorable day into a shadow box display, complete with a nice photo of the two of us, the spent brass and the coyote skull.

The skulls of animals also make unique pieces to immortalize a hunt. I have been collecting cleaned animal skulls for years and I have a representative piece of every animal I've ever hunted. I process the skulls myself, utilizing colonies of dermestid beetles that

I've cultured for almost fifteen years. After some slight processing, the skull is dried a bit and placed into the colony with the beetles. Within a few days, depending on the size of the skull, the beetle larvae will have removed every single piece of meat from the bone. The skull is then whitened using hydrogen peroxide and allowed to dry in the sun. After the whitening and drying process is complete, the skull is ready for display.

Since skull cleaning is usually a part of my hunting process, it didn't take any time at all for the girls to catch on. Starting with their very first animals, they both wanted to start their own skull collection. Both Alyssa and Jessica have the skulls of the first animals they've ever taken as licensed hunters decorating the shelves of their room. It didn't matter if it was a mourning dove or mule deer; whatever they hunted, they wanted a skull trophy to remember their hunts. Their growing collection has become a source of pride for both of them, and gives them a feeling of accomplishment.

When milestones were reached, I will admit that it was tough not to go overboard when attempting to memorialize their success. When Alyssa shot her first coyote, we were both convinced that we needed to have a full body mount done. After we investigated the cost and the practicality, we settled for a tanned pelt and a cleaned skull.

Another great way to commemorate your kid's involvement in anything outdoors is to enter their photographs in local photo contests. Several of the outdoor magazines and newspapers here in California routinely put on photo contests to encourage kids to get involved in the outdoors. Parents can send in digital photos of their children participating in any outdoor activity and winners are posted monthly. Your kids can win prizes or gift cards, but more importantly, they get to see their photograph in print. When I was a kid, getting your picture in the local newspaper or a magazine was a major badge of pride, and I don't think that's changed.

Photo submissions don't just have to be for contests. One of our outdoor papers, Western Outdoor News, frequently requests photos of all kinds from subscribers to print in their weekly periodical. Whenever my daughters had a memorable trip, I'd snap a few good photos and send them in. When the weekly paper was delivered, the girls would hover around as we leafed through it looking for their photos. Sometimes we didn't have to look through the paper at all. On a handful of occasions the editors of the paper found the submitted photos good enough for the cover. One of my favorites is a photo of Alyssa and Jessica after a 2015 dove hunt. Both my daughters requested a framed enlargement of that cover for their rooms.

It doesn't matter what you do to commemorate your time outside with your kids. If you take the time to immortalize the occasion, they'll appreciate the effort. Whether it's a nice framed photo or saving the brass from that first kill, parents should definitely go above and beyond when it comes to celebrating those early accomplishments. Our unique way of marking the occasion has started a rather unique family hunting tradition.

If you have a specific routine that you use to remember your time outside, don't be surprised if your kids copy your method and make it their own. No matter what my daughters wanted to do to remember their time outside with me, I supported and encouraged their efforts. Kids love to make you proud, and if you make a big deal of their hunting accomplishments, I believe they will strive to get better and will stay interested in the shooting sports.

On-line forums

One beneficial thing the internet has brought to our computer screens is the ability to link people with common interests from all over the world. Almost as soon as it debuted, on-line clubs or forums began to form. It doesn't matter what interest you may have, you can usually find an on-line club to join.

I started getting involved with on-line hunting or outdoor forums in about 2002. The topic boards are diverse and filled with good information. It also enabled me to meet some really good hunting partners that shared my interest and were local to where I lived. This was how I met Rito and Jose. Without this technology, I never would've met these individuals.

These types of on-line gathering spots are most definitely for adults and usually have age minimums for signing up. That doesn't mean you can't share the success of you and your kids in the field. In fact, most of the members really enjoyed seeing the on-line stories describing the girls' hunts. These types of sites were also a great way for me to show my daughters that there were people just like us all over the world that enjoyed hunting.

Even when the girls reached the age requirement for many of the on-line hunting sites, I decided that they weren't quite ready to have their own accounts. They mostly watched over my shoulder while I bounced around the different threads, or just checked the responses to their posts. This was a personal choice. I just felt that it was best that I monitor their use of these types of forums and that we viewed them as a group. To be honest, they never approached me about joining these on-line clubs, which also played into my decision to keep it a family affair.

Another huge benefit of the forums was the overwhelming camaraderie displayed by other hunters when I shared the stories of my daughters. Many members were extremely supportive and encouraging about every level of this journey. The support was refreshing and reinforced my original decision to train my girls to be hunters.

One of the forums I belong to has a tremendous world-wide following and asks its members to keep the forum active by posting new stories. To encourage this, the forum administrators run monthly contests for all forum members. Every month several stories submitted by the members are picked for Hunter of the Month honors. For a few weeks the forum participants vote on which story they think is the best. Monthly winners are announced and sent prizes. At the end of the year, the twelve monthly winners are put up for a Hunter of the Year vote. The winner of that contest receives some great prizes supplied to the forum by advertising sponsors.

For the first few forum years, I didn't even know the contests existed until a member sent me a PM and said he was voting for Alyssa's story. I clicked the link and realized she was up for Hunter of the Month honors. After winning the monthly contest, she went on to win Hunter of the Year honors in 2010, taking home a brand new Savage rifle. A year later, she came in second for the annual vote and won a nice electronic caller. A single story I posted about Jessica's first coyote took top honors in the Hunter of the year contest in 2013 and she won a rifle as well.

I don't participate in the hunting forums to enter contests. I enjoy the diverse posts, the vast experience and the camaraderie. The attention and the prizes the girls received were heartwarming and humbling. It definitely made my daughters realize that a large group of people from all over the country supported their passion and direction. After their wins, both came to me separately, stating that they'd like to see other forum members get a chance to win something.

On-line forums are great for assisting young hunters with advice. The cross section of experience on many of these sites is vast and most are more than willing to help new hunters out. They are great places to hone hunting techniques and maybe meet some hunting partners. I think joining on-line hunting forums is a great family activity that will illustrate just how popular our hunting heritage is, and how deep that interest runs.

The fox caller

The forums allowed my daughters to experience an expanded hunting culture that they had no idea existed. The camaraderie and support was refreshing, and the members were always kind and encouraging. Truth be told, it was the forum crowd that made me realize that our journey needed to be documented and shared. Almost weekly, I'd get an email or a personal message from a forum member asking for advice on getting kids involved in the outdoors. My suggestion was always the same; just take them.

Most of my forum time was spent on predator hunting forums. This brought me into contact with quite a few individuals that built their own hand calls. I had accumulated quite a few over the years, but most of those were commercially produced. I really had no idea how many hunters produced their own unique predator hand calls.

The forum members had become used to seeing Alyssa pictured on my routine hunting reports. After a few stories featuring my daughter, one of the members sent me a message and asked me if he could send me something. He said he made Alyssa something that he thought she could use. A few days later a small package arrived addressed to Alyssa. I opened it up and found a pink, laminated hand call. The call was attached to a lanyard and the note inside stated that the call was made specifically for Alyssa. The maker said that he found it admirable that I was taking my daughter hunting and he hoped that Alyssa could use the call on a hunt.

Anxious to use her new call, I took Alyssa on a late afternoon hunt near our home. For the last several years I had been exploring areas to hunt close to where I lived. After a bit of exploring, I found a spot that seemed to hold quite a few gray fox. During the season, I'd load up my gear after work and head out to make 1-2 stands before it got dark. Since the spot was close, I decided to take Alyssa to the fox spot so she could try out her new call.

Here in California, you can only use hand calls to hunt gray fox. With her brand new call hanging around her neck it was time to let Alyssa call the stand.

Alyssa had seen me use several hand calls before and she had practiced several times on multiple calls. After some pointers, she began to produce some really good sounds. Within minutes of receiving her custom call, she was filling the house with high pitched, simulated screaming, and it sounded really good.

At the spot, we quietly hiked in and got set up. We were seated at the top of a hill looking over a small, overgrown canyon. Despite the thick cover, we were set up with a great view of a couple of open areas that intersected about thirty feet below us. From where we were, anything coming to the call would need to move through these open shooting lanes.

Alyssa was sitting right next me wearing her camo jacket, brand new pink call in hand. With the confined calling area and the thick vegetation, I decided on the shotgun. I looked over at Alyssa and gave her a nod. She returned the gesture and started filling the canyon with blood-curdling death. The sun had dropped behind the ridge and the wind was still. I knew something was going to happen.

Alyssa would blow the call for about thirty seconds or so and rest. The silence was eerie. During the breaks we'd search the thick brush for movement. We were losing light quickly and within minutes we'd have to end the stand and head home.

Alyssa had just started calling again when I spotted movement to my right. I saw a flash of cinnamon-colored fur cutting through the brush. Faster than I could raise the shotgun, the gray fox appeared in the open space below us. I froze. He looked up at us and instantly ducked back into the bushes. When I spotted him cutting through the gap again, I fired into the open space, but it was too dark to see if I connected. Alyssa had spotted him in the opening, but had lost sight of the fox when he turned to leave. We decided to end the stand before it got too dark.

As the light faded, I worked my way down to the open area and searched the brush. At first I didn't find anything. Then I spotted a fluffy tail deep in the shadow of the bushes. On her first trip out, Alyssa called in a gray fox with her brand new call.

We took some great photos of our success and headed home. The next day I sent the call maker a note and told him what happened. I also posted our success on the forum, and gave full credit to the forum member that sent my daughter the call. He sent me a message saying he was honored to have Alyssa use his call. Two years later, a second call arrived in the mail for Jessica.

That area and that stand are very special for a few reasons. For three years in a row Alyssa and I would go to this spot on the exact same day every year. It became our tradition and every year we'd see or shoot a fox. It became known as the fox spot, and until a fire ravaged the area, it was our favorite place to go. Before it burned, every Valentine's Day, no matter what, Alyssa and I would make a point to be at the fox spot. On this day I like to remember all the good times I've had as a boy exploring, and how I slowly became a hunter. And on my dad's birthday, I like to be outside and think of him.

Setting up for success

When I began to notice that my daughters wanted to move beyond just target shooting, I started thinking more about how I could transition them from shooting static targets, to hunting success. I knew that they could benefit from my years of hunting experience, but I struggled a bit on the most efficient way to make this transition. Eventually it came down to simply showing them all the subtle things I do when I started taking them out hunting with me.

While I love all types of hunting, calling predators is by far one of my favorite things to do. I love the challenge, the increased opportunities and the thrill of fooling some of the smartest animals on the planet. Almost twenty years of chasing predators has helped me become a better overall hunter and a better shot. The fast action and very brief shot opportunities have taught me quick target acquisition and have sharpened my offhand shooting. In my opinion, predator hunting allows hunters to repeatedly focus on several important skills over a typical ten-stand day that apply to all types of hunting. Scent control, marksmanship, alertness and noise control are all important aspects of hunting no matter what game you're chasing. I think making repeatable stands and the increased shot opportunities provided my daughters with a somewhat accelerated course in all these hunting preparedness skills.

The two most important things I pay attention to when I prepare to make a calling stand are wind direction and elevation. Wind direction in any type of hunting is important to note, and even more so when calling predators. Coyotes will usually circle downwind when responding to a call. Prior to calling, a hunter would benefit from understanding where the wind is blowing his scent.

Picking a sitting spot with a bit of elevation will allow hunters to spot approaching predators coming to the call. Spotting an animal before they spot you is a huge benefit that tips the advantage to the hunter. In simple terms, I like to sit where I can see. I make sure I'm not sky lined when I sit down and I try to sit in the shadows of vegetation or at least in front of brush to break up my outline.

I use both hand calls and electronic calls when I hunt predators. I believe both have their advantages, and I usually have both types with me on every stand I make. Hand calls are simple and convenient, and in my opinion, work just as good as electronic callers. They don't require batteries, you can start calling as soon as you find a spot to sit, and with a little practice, they most definitely will call in the critters.

Today's market is absolutely flooded with high quality, digital calls. Many hold far more sounds than a typical hunter will ever need and they usually have more bells and whistles than I think is necessary. Almost all the electronic calls on the market come with a remote that allows the hunter to change volume and sound from a distance. The advantage here is that the source of the sound can be placed in a different location, drawing the attention away from the hunter.

When I walk out to place the electronic caller, I'm very specific on where I put it. Despite the insane remote ranges now available on some callers, I rarely set my caller more than 50-75 yards away from my shooting perch. I understand that every step I take is moving my scent across my calling area and I like to minimize this as much as possible. I keep it close and simple.

Once I find where I want to place the caller, I check the wind at this location. I can't tell you how many times I've checked the wind direction where I'm set up, only to have it be different down at the call. I like to place the caller favoring the upwind side giving me lots of room right in front should an animal circle downwind of the call.

While I'm at the caller, I take a quick second and glance back to my set up spot. I do this to make sure that I'm hidden and to assure that nothing out of the ordinary can be spotted by an approaching predator. This is a great tactic to make absolutely sure that you and your hunting partner blend in to your surroundings. When I return to where I'll be sitting after placing the caller, I walk back on the same exact path I used to walk in. In my mind, doing this will minimize my sent trail. I'm not sure if it works, but it's now an old habit I refuse to break.

Once I sit down, I get my rifle and sticks set up. As with the previous steps, I have a specific way of doing this as well. Being a right handed shooter, it is more comfortable for me to swing my firearm from right to left on a target. Moving my set up from left to right feels uncomfortable and is not a quality shooting platform for me. If you need an example, try this. Sit on the floor with your back against a couch, legs perpendicular to the sofa. Now pretend you're shouldering your rifle. Slowly rotate left and right. Depending on your dominant hand, you'll feel far more comfortable moving one way rather than the other. And let's be honest, when you're comfortable, you shoot better.

On absolutely every stand, without fail, I will set up facing as far to the right as I can, giving me almost 180 degrees of comfortable movement from right to left. I like to sit in the shadows, so I'll place my right shoulder up close to whatever is casting that shadow. It almost looks like I am favoring the right side over the left while calling. In reality, I am setting up so that if anything approaches in front of me, left or right, I can quickly and comfortably rotate my gear and put the crosshairs on fur.

If I need to move, instead of rotating my upper body to move into position, I maintain a rigid connection with my rifle and sticks, and use my rear end as the pivot point. Kind of like a turret on a tank, turning all at once to get on target quickly. If I stay in essentially the same position behind the rifle, I can acquire my target faster because my overall position is repeatable and changes very little.

Once my spot is picked, I take a few seconds to clear out the area where I'm sitting. I'll push away leaf litter, remove sticks and rocks, and make sure that any movement I may make to adjust to an approaching predator will not be impeded by anything. This is a huge advantage in escaping detection. I also quietly move my sticks and rifle from right to left, and then back again, making sure the area is clear. I believe anything you can do during your set up that will tip the odds in your favor, is worth doing.

Just before I start calling, I check my variable scope setting. I rotate it down to a lower magnification in case I call something in close. Being used to my gear, I know which way to rotate it should I need to take a shot at distance without even looking down at the rifle.

I also glance around my calling area and pick out some paths or shooting corridors. Most animals like to use paths or openings in terrain just like we do. I find these pathways and pay attention to them during the calling.

Lastly, this type of hunting requires your focused attention the entire time you're calling. You should be on edge and alert the whole time you're on stand. Predators coming to the call can come in fast and aggressive. I've heard growling and heavy panting as coyotes race within feet of me. I've shot coyotes so close to my position that it left me with blood and ravenous saliva on my boots. Hunters should be ready to pull the trigger as soon the calling starts. To give you an idea, several years ago I had a coyote show up seven seconds after I started calling.

Incorporating these techniques into my calling sequence allows me to quickly acquire targets and gives me the confidence to make good shots and harvest more predators. These skills of course translate to any type of hunting. Using these preparation techniques no matter what you're chasing, will definitely give any hunter an edge. These subtle steps will teach your youth patience, and will illustrate that doing a little extra preparation will lead to more hunting success. It doesn't matter if you chase predators or not, these steps should sharpen your outdoor hunting skills.

Using her shooting sticks, Jessica practicing safe muzzle management during a pig hunt (Hovey 2015).

Jessica getting some trigger time behind the Taurus .357 loaded with .38 rounds. During early pistol training, I stayed close to keep things safe (Hovey 2014).

Alyssa and Jessica turning their backs, demonstrating safe field loading (Hovey 2015).

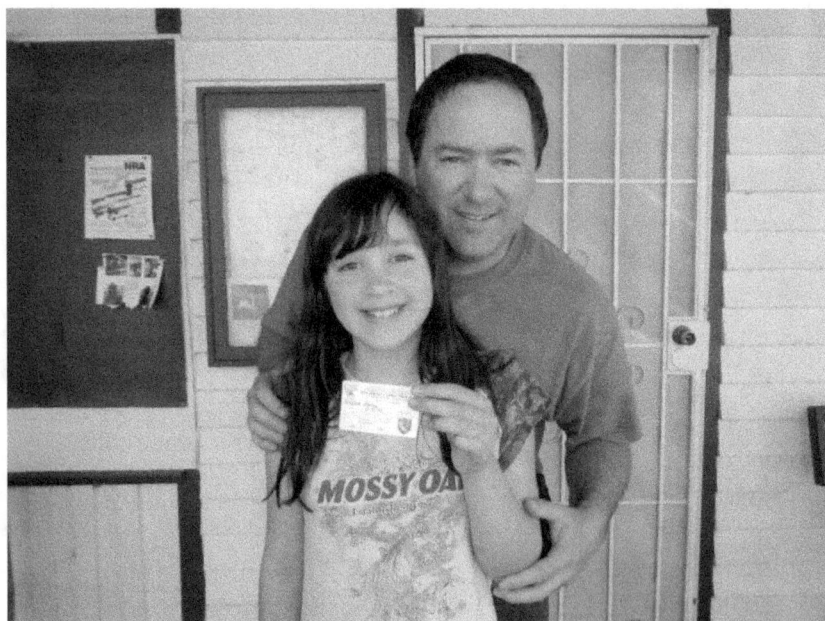

Jessica with her hard-earned hunter's safety card. Taking the course with your kids, or attending the training with them, will make the process easier on them (Hovey 2013).

Alyssa and Jessica sharing a dove field with Carly Mattila (C), a friend since grade school (Hovey 2015).

A great dove hunt with Jose and Adrian De Orta. Shooting with friends builds camaraderie and strong memories. Involving other kids interested in the shooting sports during this process turned out to be very rewarding (Hovey 2014).

Jose and Adrian De Orta target shooting in the desert. Training our kids in the shooting sports at the same time provided countless benefits and memories (Hovey 2014).

Jessica learning basic driving skills in the wide open desert. Both my daughters learned to drive my truck long before they were of legal driving age. In remote areas, I wanted them to be able to drive in case of an emergency (Hovey 2015).

Alyssa got plenty of practice changing tires over the course of this journey. It was important for me to teach them how to take care of issues on their own, just like my dad had taught me (Hovey 2012).

Alyssa showing nothing but concentration at the CrossFit gym. Her dedication to her fitness at her age amazes me (Hovey 2016).

Jessica performing a split-jerk at the CrossFit gym. Beyond the physical strength, the self confidence my daughters gained being part of an organized fitness program assisted in building their character and self esteem (Hovey 2016).

The Angry Baker field dressing a cottontail rabbit. From the field to the table, Jessica discovered her culinary creativity with wild game she herself hunted (Hovey 2015).

Varying the angle of your digital camera and using the flash will definitely enhance your outdoor photos. To capture this amazing sunset, I placed the camera low for this photograph and used the flash for a dramatic effect (Hovey 2005).

Using a tripod I've taken some great digital photos when I hunt by myself. Digital technology has completely revolutionized outdoor photography (Hovey 2009).

Take a few minutes to make sure the animal looks clean and free of excess blood. The captured moment shouldn't look gory, just memorable (Hovey 2009).

NORTHERN CALIFORNIA'S *ONLY* SPORTSMAN'S WEEKLY

Volume 63, Number 37/September 11, 2015

WESTERN OUTDOOR NEWS

More kings are moving *into the* ***Sacramento River,*** **See p1**

Dove opener fantastic but short-lived!

Red Bluff upriver the focus for improved salmon action
Page 1

Salmon run up 'salmon highway' into Bay
Page 1

$3.25 U.S.

THE DOVE OPENER was excellent almost everywhere, Page 1

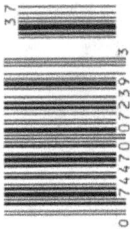

WHITE SEABASS came from Pt. Reyes, Page 1

A simple photo submission to Western Outdoor News resulted in an awesome cover shot for Alyssa and Jessica (Hovey 2015).

Alyssa's handmade predator call made for her by a hunting forum member. Once other hunters realized my daughters were interested in hunting, the calls kept coming (Hovey 2008).

On her first trip out with her new call, Alyssa called in this Valentine's Day fox for me. It didn't matter what type of hunting I was doing, Alyssa always wanted to go (Hovey 2008).

TALKING POINTS

I believe it's never too early for kids to learn that what we do as hunters is completely supported by science, is critical to the health of the resource and is an activity that they should be proud to participate in. I tell both my daughters that they should never apologize for being hunters and that when they get into discussions of the activity, they should take the high road and attempt to educate the uninformed.

Knowledge is power and the best way to communicate a sportsmen's point of view to those that'll listen, is to politely present them with hard facts. There is a tremendous amount of data demonstrating the complete dedication and devotion to the resource by sportsmen. Data on species recovery numbers and sportsmen contributions throughout the recent history of hunting in America shows that sportsmen are true conservationists. Using sound science and a proven wildlife conservation model, these facts are impossible to dispute. This solid resource preservation example is and will forever be the crowning legacy of all outdoorsmen.

In a culture where firearms are vilified and animals are humanized and given names, it becomes difficult to see the scientific truth through the tangle of emotion. However, once the fog of the ignorant dissipates, the pillars of support are always science and they are always there.

Confused by nature

I was born here in California and have resided in the Golden State my entire life. I love the climate, the easy access to the coast and the mountains, and all the opportunities afforded me over a lifetime of residency. After briefly entertaining relocating somewhere else, my wife and I decided that California is where we belong. Despite these benefits, it has been my experience that there is a severe disconnection here between the suburban masses and nature.

Many here have little to no experience with the outside world and have even less of an understanding of resource management. They essentially know little about the role hunting plays in maintaining healthy animal populations and few have ever experienced the taste of wild meat. For many, the concept of acquiring their protein, starts and ends at the back of the store in the meat section.

Years ago I was at the back of our local super market perusing the pork chop selection. A woman wheeled her cart to the adjacent meat section and began her search for just the right cut. In her cart was a young girl of about four years old. As she shopped, the little girl began to comment about the massive wall of meat in front of her. "Wow, this is a lot of meat!" she said. I had to agree. I looked up and down the counter and tried to envision just how many animals worth of protein were neatly cut and packaged here in front of me.

The mother was focused on her task and politely agreed with her daughter. The little girl's next comment required an answer. "Where does all this meat come from?" she asked. Without even thinking about it, the mom stated that the meat was cut up and packaged in the back of the store for the customers. I guess for most little kids that answer would've been enough. For the most part, the mother's answer wasn't incorrect. However, the little girl wasn't satisfied with the response.

"Yeah, but where does all the meat COME from?" she demanded. A slight smile crossed my face as I knew that we were now at the crossroads of this brief conversation. The mother settled on a cut and grabbed the neatly wrapped package of four pork chops, splayed out like thick, meaty playing cards and placed it in her cart. She smoothed down her daughter's hair and gave her an answer I'll remember for the rest of my life. "Oh sweetie, they make the meat in the back of the store and bring it out here after it's packaged." She glanced my way and gave me a plastic smile. She then pushed her cart, her pork chops and her misinformed daughter down the aisle.

As I left, I thought about how the woman's simple answer had done far more harm than good. I didn't feel it was my place to correct the woman, but I couldn't help but think that an opportunity to educate the young girl had been missed.

Along with the confusion on the origin of supermarket meat, many Californians are also very unaware of exactly how nature works. They feel a connection with the outside world when they actively head out to view wildlife, which is good. However, viewing is only a small portion of nature, and when predator and prey tangle in front of the viewing public, things can get a little confusing for them.

The California coast is a migratory corridor for many species of whales. During certain times of the year, people will head out on whale watching cruises hoping to get a glimpse of the large marine mammals. It was during one of these popular cruises where the paying customers got a front row seat on how nature really works.

Early in the trip, the boat captain spotted a mother gray whale and her newborn calf just off the coast. California gray whales will come very close to shore during their migration to feed near the kelp beds. The pair was about a mile from shore and appeared to be lazily moving north. Dozens of watchers pulled out their video cameras and started filming the whales as they slowly swam near the surface. The captain could be heard narrating the natural history of the gray whale on several of the video clips. The passengers could also be heard on the clip enjoying the sighting. It was very clear that all aboard were in whale watching bliss. That is, until the predators showed up.

A small pod of killer whales or orcas quickly circled the pair of grays and instantly started trying to separate mother and calf. At first the uneducated crowd thought the Sea World whales were playing with the pair. They could not have been more wrong.

The larger bulls could be seen ramming the mother, pushing her from the calf. Once the orcas separated the grays, two killer whales began pushing the calf below the water in attempts to drown it. The actions were violent and purposeful. Another killer whale began biting the fluke of the calf and pulling it below the surface. Shades of crimson soon surrounded the scene and the crowd's mood suddenly changed.

Some could be heard openly weeping on the clip as they realize the orcas were trying to kill the calf. A woman in the background, voice quivering with sadness, demanded that the captain call the Coast Guard so they can put a stop to the attack. The order can be heard several times on the clip until the captain finally explains that they are not to intervene in any way.

This clip illustrates the complete disconnect that many have between an occasional encounter with nature and what nature is truly capable of. It appears that many are content to view and comprehend only the happy side of nature. But when things turn dark, and they always will, they shield their eyes and conclude that this side is wrong and bad. Or they believe that at the very least, Nature needs to be issued a citation by the Coast Guard.

This confusion doesn't just come from many turning their backs on the violent side of nature. It's also present in how many view the natural behaviors of many species, some inherently dangerous, that exist around us.

Mountain lions have been a protected species here in California since the early 1990's. Misinformed on just about every aspect of the lion's life history, population status and predatory behavior, the California people voted to protect the mountain lion and remove it from the species of game managed through hunting here in the state.

Now, with absolutely no fear of man, these large cats view us as an occasional food source. Here's an example of how the uneducated public can see protecting the California mountain lion as a good thing, but the existing data suggests otherwise.

Between 1890 and 1985 there were three attacks on humans by mountain lions here in California. Unfortunately, all three of these attacks resulted in the death of the victims; two of those (1909) were by the same lion with rabies, whose victims died of the disease, not the attack. This data shows that in almost 100-years, only three people have been attacked by mountain lions in California. During this period, mountain lions were actively managed through hunting, and the human population was a fraction of what it is today.

In 1990, the people of California voted to approve Proposition 117, which placed the mountain lion on a protected list, making it unlawful to pursue, hunt or possess in the Golden State. This means that since 1990, mountain lions began to no longer fear man as a predator and started to consider them prey. Since the California population of mountain lions is no longer being actively managed by the state through hunting, the cougar population continues to grow, with no new territory available to this increasing population. Young mountain lions, ready to forage on their own, must now search the rural and in some cases suburban edges looking for prey. This puts new segments of the mountain lion population into direct contact with humans. As California's human population continues to grow, and mountain lion numbers increase, more negative interactions or attacks have occurred.

From 1986 to 2014 between fifteen and twenty mountain lion attacks on humans have occurred here in California (the numbers vary on the validity of several of these attacks due to unconfirmed documentation of the injuries). The California Department of Fish and Wildlife recognizes fifteen attacks as being confirmed during this time period.

A combination of an increasing human population and an increasing, unmanaged mountain lion population here in California has created a severe imbalance that is only going to get worse. Add in the public's complete lack of information on mountain lion behavior and natural history, and close encounters will not only become more numerous, but dangerous.

A case in point is a 2014 news report of a cougar taking up residents in the basement of a house in the Hollywood Hills. The mountain lion gained access through an open window and was discovered by a service man rewiring the residence. When I heard how the lion was discovered, I thought how the maintenance man should consider himself very lucky that he wasn't attacked.

After several attempts to capture the mountain lion failed, agency personnel left the scene to let the cougar escape on its own. A day later, the radio-collared lion left the basement and escaped into the hills of nearby Griffith Park. The homeowner was interviewed and said she felt privileged that the mountain lion had chosen her home to rest in, and she hoped that he returns. This sentiment illustrates that most of the public see mountain lions as just large kitties that eat Kibble, rather than an animal that can clamp its jaws on the back of your skull and drag you into the brush to feed on you.

At the conclusion of the encounter, a newscaster finished up the report stating that the surrounding community was now safe since the tracking collar had shown that the cougar was 'very far away,' at a distance of a mile; a distance that could be covered by a running cougar in about three minutes.

While these types of examples are frustrating, they can be considered mere annoyances compared to the voluntary disarming of the public here in California. About twice a year, usually following some high-profile crime event, public officials, in coordination with law enforcement, will sponsor a Gun Buyback Event. If the law abiding public happens to have unwanted or unused firearms in their household and would like to get rid of them, they are instructed to bring them down to some central location and hand them over, usually in exchange for a gift card. These events are heavily publicized through the news media and are touted as 'a way to get dangerous firearms off the streets.' Believing that criminals will somehow get their hands on these closet relics, the public will usually comply. In reality, all these events succeed in doing is to disarm an already passive public.

I often wonder what these individuals, now armed with nothing more than a plastic gift card, plan to purchase with their new found windfall. One can only hope it goes towards a security system for their home.

Last year, during one of these events, a newscaster was interviewing people that were participating in the voluntary pacification. The reporter approached a vehicle in line waiting to surrender their firearms. She asked the gentleman behind the wheel why he was there. He stated that he had three rifles in the trunk that have been sitting in his closet for thirty years. In his words, he said he was there to hand them over so he could get them off the streets! Even the newscaster found this statement peculiar, since he had just mentioned that the rifles had sat idle in his closet for three decades.

If this public disarming isn't bad enough, the mentality towards firearms here in California is so distorted that I've even seen

Toy Gun Buyback Events. In my opinion, these events are as bad as the actual firearm surrenders. These events attempt to train, not only parents, but children that anything that even looks like a gun is bad.

The principles behind the plastic buyback are still the same. Parents whose children have been given toy guns can turn them over in exchange for a gift card. The local news had of course participated in covering the buyback and had featured a clip of the event at the beginning of the newscast. The short film panned the crowd waiting in line to hand over their plastic implements of death. I caught myself laughing as the last guy in line was holding three, cartoon-like Super Soaker water guns.

I wish I could say these examples are unique. The truth is I see this type of stuff out here in California almost every day. With this happy and fluffy view of wildlife, and this dark and twisted view of firearms, you can only imagine how the activity of hunting is viewed here in California. The truth is, if I didn't actively seek out those that also hunted, I would not have a single example of anyone in my family or neighborhood that was a hunter.

Let's talk science

As a biologist and an avid sportsman, I understand how my participation in hunting game animals assists in the management of that species. To maintain a consistently healthy population of these animals, your state resource agency, through sound science, sets limits and seasons so that all game populations remain healthy and sustainable. It doesn't matter what life history aspect you're talking about, all the information used to manage any resource effectively is done with science gathered by biologists.

Almost all states use the North American Model of Wildlife Conservation to manage the resources of their state. With strong sportsmen support, the framework of this concept began to form in the 1860's, with a firm foundation of conservation and wildlife management. The two basic principles of this model are; fish and wildlife are for the non-commercial use of citizens, and those resources should be managed such that they are available at optimum population levels forever.

This last principle refers to maintaining what is called a sustainable yield of the resource. This means that whatever is taken out of the population by sportsmen, accidental death or disease is replaced through species reproduction every season.

The absolute best way to maintain a sustainable yield of any given resource is to use hunting to manage that resource. Game managers establish this balance with the help of outdoorsmen. Set seasons and limits are verified through tag validation and end-of-the-season enumeration. If the number of a species killed during a specified season is less than expected, they can evaluate the health of the population and adjust accordingly. This type of game species data would be almost impossible to collect without hunters.

Maintaining a fairly regular level of game numbers keeps a given population healthier than if it was left fallow and un-hunted. Keeping stocks level and adjusting take numbers through hunting, reduces the possibility of disease and will assure that sufficient habitat and forage for continued generations of game species is available.

The North American Model of Wildlife Conservation has proven to not only be a successful model for resource management, it also illustrates the valuable contribution sportsmen have made to the health of game species across the country. These facts will not change and hunters need to embrace and support their valuable role.

Out here in California, we've already seen what happens when you remove game species from hunting consideration. The public voted to label the mountain lion 'protected' and have it removed from the list of hunted game animals here in California. This wasn't about preservation or diminished population numbers. This was about a voting public that knew nothing of the natural behavior of the mountain lion.

Science has shown that an adult cougar will kill one deer a week during its lifetime. With a lifespan in the wild of anywhere from eight to twelve years, a single healthy lion can kill over 500 deer in their lifetime. With an estimated population here in California of

4,000 to 6,000 mountain lions, simple fourth grade math clearly illustrates that the numbers are seriously stacked against the deer population. This has resulted in a severe resource management imbalance. We have effectively protected the predator and continue to manage the prey, the California deer, for take. You can just imagine what that does to the deer population in this state.

The science behind these management principles involves understanding the life histories of all game species, and establishing hunting seasons so that species are not harassed during critical portions of their life history. The most important life history stage in managing game animals is when species breed. The breeding season drives the hunting season. Hunting is not allowed during the time animals are breeding, pregnant or actively raising their young. All game species are managed so that animals killed by hunters do not substantial reduced the population beyond what is replaced by the species reproducing.

Following sound science we can actively hunt game species in this country, providing meat for the freezer, and do so without negatively impacting the population. Sportsmen are also crucial in keeping the populations at a level where they never overpopulate an area, negatively impacting their habitat. Lastly, maintaining game species at a consistent level keeps individuals healthy and overall disease free, so everyone, even those that don't hunt, can enjoy them in perpetuity. This takes dedication and hard work, and all of the sportsmen and women of this country do this unselfishly.

Educating those with no experience

I think some out there that aren't familiar with shooting or firearms are simply afraid of what they don't know about. I completely understand this and I make it a point to try and educate those that have questions whenever I can. I hear non-shooters say all the time that they'd like to get into hunting or shooting, but they aren't sure how to get started. Let's face it this isn't like jumping into other activities without experience. I think the general public is probably afraid of hunting and the shooting sports because it involves firearms.

I have always viewed all firearms as nothing more than tools for a specific action. I was raised to do the best I can at fixing things myself, and becoming familiar with your tools is vital to staying safe and getting the job done correctly. Most of us know not to grab a hammer by the head and to swing the handle. I view my familiarity with firearms no differently. They are tools that I can use to fill my freezer, recreate and protect myself. They are not the evil symbols of hate or possessed items that kill indiscriminately. They are inanimate objects that if left alone, will do nothing more than rust and corrode. The actions of that tool are only achieved by the person holding it. Just like with the hammer. Teaching new shooters this obvious metaphor should ease their misguided fears. Taking them out to experience a fun day on the range, will further demonstrate, that when done safely, shooting is an enjoyable and rewarding activity.

Out here in southern California, there are a number of shooting ranges located within an hour's drive of Los Angeles. If you know someone that is interested in shooting but hesitant, a shooting range is the best place to start. Some offer instructional guidance to assist a new shooter and the structured atmosphere will emphasize safety. Some ranges are more organized than others, so pick one that will make a strong safety impression on the new shooter. The range I take my daughters to is run with a strict adherence to safety and all shooters are obliged to follow the range safety protocol or they'll be escorted from the property. In my opinion, when it comes to gun safety and shooting next to strangers, I would rather see strict rules that teach new shooters the correct way to handle firearms, to set the right example at the beginning of their training.

When I encounter someone that is curious about shooting or the outdoors, I always try to figure out how I can help them get to the next level. Whether it's taking them to a shooting range, suggesting they take a hunter's safety course, or taking them on their first hunt, I feel it's the obligation of all sportsmen to spend a little time and effort to get others interested in the activity we love. Getting others involved will benefit everyone.

Why I hunt

As a lifelong California hunter, I've had to deal with my fair share of questions on why I hunt. The inquiries have ranged from genuine curiosity to those bordering on righteous rudeness from the misinformed and uneducated. I always find the specific question a bit humorous..."why do you hunt?" If you asked anyone that question a hundred years ago, the answer would be simple; we hunt to eat.

In my opinion, our society has not only drifted from the concept of gathering our own food, but we've essentially turned our backs on it. So much so, that those that still hunt to fill their freezer, are regarded as barbaric and worst of all cruel. In my opinion, those that don't educate themselves on where their food comes from are far crueler than a hunter that puts wild meat in his freezer.

Those that eat meat and don't hunt should understand that the money they use to purchase that meat goes to paying someone to kill that animal for them. Just because they're removed from the process, doesn't mean they aren't part of it. They've essentially hired an assassin to kill for them. The flesh of that animal, so neatly and uniformly placed in the super market display case, was once alive. When it comes right down to it, their money funded the death of that animal and hopefully they understand that. So, who can be considered crueler, the hunter that goes out and hunts for their own wild meat, or the non-hunter that blindly pays someone else to do the dirty work for them?

As hunters, we're part of the process from beginning to end. We understand that our role is to find the animal and to kill efficiently. No self respecting hunter wants any animal to suffer. They practice their craft, and become quick killers. They choose their shots wisely and concentrate on making a clean, quick kill.

When the animal is down, we approach it humbly and with respect. I've taught my daughters to take a few minutes to admire the creature and revere it. I tell them to think about how they are the first humans to ever touch the animal, and for that, we should be thankful.

When I pull out the knives, I take my time and prepare the meat with care. I harvest whatever I can and make sure I take care of the meat and keep it clean. After it cools, I pack it out in meat bags. Once home, I cut it into single portions, vacuum pack the meat and place it in the freezer.

From finding my prey in the wild, to having individually packed meat portions in my freezer, I am involved in every step of gathering and preparing that food. When I put that meat on my family's plate, I know exactly where that food came from, and what it took to get it to the table.

My daughters have been right at my side helping when I get an animal on the ground. They've also cleaned and quartered their own animals ever since they've started. They understand that pulling the trigger is only part of the entire process. They know that at times, if we want to eat, we hunt.

Since the very beginning I have stressed to my daughters how our hunting activity helps the resource. I have shown them that every animal we hunt is to be respected and admired. I have explained that even though we hunt, we are the true defenders of the wildlife. Most importantly, I've taught them to be proud hunters.

When they got a little older, their friends and acquaintances began asking them why they hunted. I taught Alyssa and Jessica to either politely educate those that will listen or to ignore those that won't. From about second grade on, my daughters have worn camo to school. Since no one else their age hunted, they quickly became known as the hunter girls. That label was fine by me. But if those generic labels became hurtful or misguided, I let the girls know that they should ignore the ignorant and guide the misguided.

Long before I first took my daughters target shooting, I had to decide for myself if taking them on this journey was a good idea. I knew teaching them the shooting sports and ultimately how to hunt in California was going against the publically perceived moral grain. It wasn't enough for me to say that I didn't care what others thought, and I don't. However, I wanted to make sure that I didn't impose any unnecessary drama on my daughters just because I wanted to teach them how to hunt.

At times it has been a struggle. Both my daughters have grown up in the social media world and, like typical teenagers, communicate with friends and family using several of the more popular social media outlets. When they had successful hunting adventures, and inevitably wanted to share their success by posting photos, I will admit I cringed a bit. However, something rather surprising began to occur when my girls started posting hunting photos and stories.

While they did have a few detractors that voiced their ignorance with no attempt to understand, most of their friends were supportive and, believe it or not, envious. Several of their friends even inquired about how to get started. Two of Jessica's teachers wanted to try venison jerky should her next deer hunt be successful.

As we move through this experience, I find that I've learned a great deal as well. The most important lessons I've learned is to never hide your passion, never apologize for your interest and the more you educate those that may not fully understand the better off our heritage will be. In short, you should never feel like you're doing anything wrong when you head out to hunt.

Why do I hunt? It's challenging, enjoyable and legal. It keeps me in shape. It provides meat for my family, and gives me a connection to the outside world that non-hunters will never understand. To be perfectly honest, in my mind, there is no downside to hunting.

Human impacts

I don't care who you are or where you live, if you live in a home and eat, you have impacted the animals around you. If you live in a house, you've disrupted just about every level of animal life, from the invertebrates that made a living in the soil now covered with cement, to the larger herbivores that use to browse the native vegetation where the foundation of your house now sits. Many don't think about this impact, or justify it as a one-time thing. In reality, that cement slab has completely removed that piece of habitat from any animal forever.

The food humans consume is grown or raised somewhere, permanently altering the habitat in these areas now converted to agriculture or grazing fields. The simple act of feeding and repeatedly trampling the ground by cattle permanently alters the terrain and any vegetation that may attempt to germinate in the grazed soil. A cattle-grazed field can sit fallow for decades and still show signs of cattle disturbance. That's a lofty price to pay for a steak.

Those that don't consume meat and choose a vegan lifestyle must understand that their dependency on plant matter for sustenance has a tremendous impact on the resource as well. The amount of pesticides, herbicides and water used to grow crops, demonstrates that even eating vegetation is far from benign. Those fields that are now forever changed due to the agriculture that puts salad on your table were once home to native plants and animals that will never roam that plot of land again. The process of harvesting these edible plants is destructive and not passive. Large machines roll down the rows of vegetables, systematically picking what you eat, simultaneously killing small mammals, snakes and lizards that frequent the field to feed on the plants or insects that are attracted to the area.

In many cases, these habitats are so altered and damaged, that even if left fallow, it would be impossible for native plants to return to this destroyed piece of soil. Non-native plants are so much more adaptable to disturbed areas, and are often the first to re-colonize an agriculture field that is no longer planted. Once an area is repeatedly farmed, it is difficult if not impossible to return it to its native state.

If you have pets, the food that you so innocently feed them was made using animal protein, again raised and grazed somewhere. Bits of chicken, fish, beef and pork are churned up and mixed with grains and binders to form the dry food your cat or dog eats. Depending on how many pets you have, this consumptive use of the domestic resource can be expensive and is a repeatable indirect impact.

Impacts don't just come from consumable products. If you look around your home, you'll see plenty of items that had a direct or somewhat indirect impact on the resource. Plastics are manufactured using petroleum, a byproduct of crude oil. Oil wells are placed on large cement paddocks, covering habitat and eliminating it for all levels of wildlife.

Clothing made with animal products like wool, cashmere or silk, are made with the byproducts of animals. However, these animals are actively farmed for these byproducts and in most cases, kept in areas with altered habitat to increase production; habitat that has been permanently changed.

Leather shoes, couches, belts or car seats all used to be living, breathing animals, and were farmed for their skin in pastures that are grazed down to bare dirt and then replaced with non-native grasses. Not to mention the impact to the animal itself.

Unless you live in a hot air balloon powered by your own waste, no one is above impacting the planet at some level. Humans have, and always will impact their environment to some extent. The best we, as a species can hope for is that we try and minimize that impact whenever and wherever we can.

Endangered animals

It constantly amazes me how little the general public knows about the species status known as endangered. Frequently, anti-hunters will instantly jump to the 'endangered' label whenever they wade into the hunting argument. They either emphatically state that the hunted animal is on the endangered species list or that the actual act of hunting is pushing that species towards extinction. Unfortunately, the use of this label by anti-hunters is mostly misused and likely tossed around to enrage the misinformed public.

The most common definition of endangered states: *An endangered species is a plant or animal species existing in such small numbers that it is in danger of becoming extinct, especially such a species placed in jeopardy as a result of human activity. One of the principal factors in the endangerment or extinction of a species is the destruction or pollution of its native habitat. Other factors include the accidental or intentional introduction of alien species that out-compete the native species for environmental resources.*

This definition describes species that are so rare that they are usually seldom seen, extremely localized and so close to completely disappearing, that federal and state agencies have listed them as very near extinction. As of October 2015, the United States Fish and Wildlife Service (USFWS), the agency responsible for listing and maintaining an endangered and threatened species list, has almost 1,600 species documented as endangered in the United States. If we break down this number, we can see how completely disconnected the label 'endangered' and the activity of hunting truly is.

Of the 1,600 species on the USFWS list, 898, over half, are flowering and non-flowering plant species. Aquatic and terrestrial invertebrates make up the next largest group with 259 species. One hundred are non-game bird species and 163 are fish species. Reptiles and amphibians make up 77 species on the list and 102 are mammal species. Of these mammal species, 50 are rabbit-sized or smaller (bats, voles, shrews, squirrels, foxes, kangaroo rats, wood rats, gophers and rabbits), and 21 are marine mammals (whales). Of the remaining 31 species (1.9 % of the entire listed species), only five species (grizzly bear, CA bighorn sheep, wolf, American bison and pronghorn) are animals that are considered in low numbers in localized areas and thus listed. However, in some states, due to proper wildlife management, these species are thriving and sportsmen are allowed to hunt them.

The label 'endangered' is tossed around haphazardly and when this term is applied to legal hunting, it is used incorrectly. Animals that are endangered are in such low numbers that they are at the gate of extinction. The diverse populations of game animals in this country are thriving and nowhere close to endangered. These populations are managed through hunting and will be around for hunters and non-hunters to enjoy for as long as quality resource management exists.

Almost all animals currently listed under the endangered status are there due to habitat loss through human encroachment. Those species that can't adapt to environmental changes, or the loss of habitat, will fail to thrive, and without successful reproduction, will eventually disappear. Hunting has nothing to do with this. In fact, hunting's support of resource management benefits many more species than those that are hunted. Habitat restoration and creation, paid for with sportsmen dollars, benefit all levels of plant and animal species that co-occur with game species. Because game species have value to hunters, the habitat preserved for that species will benefit all species hunted and non-hunted that also occur on that preserved plot of land.

Being a biologist in charge of monitoring threatened and endangered species in the southern section of California, I am very familiar with state and federal endangered species status, and the reasoning these species are listed. In no instance is the activity of hunting the reason behind their precarious status. In this country, suggesting that hunting well managed species is pushing those species towards extinction is not only preposterous, it is scientifically incorrect. One thing does not have anything to do with the other.

If we look at all species currently hunted in this country, none of them are anywhere close to endangered. Many of the species on the federal endangered list aren't considered game species and none of them are hunted. Resources are preserved when they are assigned a value. Sportsmen contribute millions of dollars to the management of game species and inadvertently preserve habitat for other species, including special status animals that also inhabit that same habitat.

The anti-hunter's violent mindset

We all have our opinions and points of view on any of a number of diverse topics. If you're an adult, you may politely argue these points with neighbors, friends or acquaintances. You provide facts usually based on science and discuss your point of view rationally. If you're passionate about your topic of choice, the discussion may get heated, but a civilized society has taught us to stay calm and to be mature. These concepts seem to be completely absent when anti-hunters discuss hunting.

We've all seen the lengths to which anti-hunters go to verbally attack any hunter that decides to celebrate their success on-line. They have a serious amount of frustration and anger that is liberally poured over the next individual that they consider the most hated person on the web. The internet has become the battle ground for the hunters that legally pursue game, and those that take great offense to this activity. I believe that the individuals that decide to attack the legal hunting community are not only clueless when it comes to resource management and the hunter's role, but they could care less.

We as hunters understand and assist in conserving the animals we hunt at a level far above that of the anti-hunter. We spend money, create habitat, follow game laws and enjoy the resource at a level that clearly demonstrates our point of view. We are secure in our beliefs, our direction and our emotions on this topic. We are supported with sound science and will continue to participate in this activity, and more importantly, pass it on to the next generation. This is a lifestyle investment, and we as hunters are willing to walk the walk to protect the resource. The anti-hunter that decides to cross that line into fanaticism will paint a few signs and stand on a street corner for a few days. Or they'll plan their attack on-line where they remain anonymous and hidden. Their investment in time is extremely low and their financial support is usually inconsistent and minimal. Their intentions are not to help the resource; their intentions are to attack the sportsman.

I believe all humans in general are animal lovers. We have domesticated animals to provide human companionship at some level, and I personally don't know of anyone that doesn't own a pet. However, these animals are pets, they eat from bowls on the ground, they pee in the yard, and while they do become parts of the family, they are still animals. When people start elevating their pets to a level that is socially and emotionally equal to humans, those individuals start to lose the importance of the human condition.

Anti-hunters frequently engage in this type of animal worship, equalizing or elevating an animal's life above that of a human. In my opinion, this mentality devalues the importance of being human. When they bring this mindset into a heated altercation with a hunter, a rational discussion with these individuals is impossible.

Now, more frequently, these types of anti-hunting/hunter altercations are being picked up by the news media. Once the hunting story gathers momentum, the media outlet could care less about the topic of the story or who hates whom. They play to the electrified emotion of the report and high emotions means good ratings. A cute story on pandas, lions or puppies, will always get the phones ringing and the viewers staying tuned. And have you noticed that only the cute animals get air time? How come no one wants to hear about hyenas, snakes and rats? That's because the segment of our culture that is willing to demean and degrade anyone that acts or thinks differently, the anti-hunters, are very selective in their approach to adoration. Cute and pretty animals will always usurp animals that the human condition has deemed ugly or nasty. These individuals are clearly operating at a level of primitive visual stimulation, and completely outside the realm of true nature or science.

As these topics trend and gain more attention from the media, the portion of our culture that are undecided on the subject, are beginning to see a very ugly and callous segment of the anti-hunting movement. The internet provides a front row seat on how these individuals operate, and I believe the general public is getting tired of it. They see these major overreactions to the legal hunting of animals, and the often barbaric and fanatical tactics this group uses. Death threats, the publishing of personal information and in some cases vandalism are all common tactics used by anti-hunters that have a completely warped sense of what an appropriate response is. While the initial mob-like salvo may froth up the internet, their continued absurd and outlandish demands for the physical harm or death of their target, is beginning to shine a very bright, unstable light on the anti-hunter.

We've all heard about the American dentist that shot the thirteen-year old African lion in the summer of 2015. To be honest, I was sick and tired of all the coverage and the attention that lasted for weeks. In the beginning, there appeared to be some questions on the ethics of the hunt. If the animal was poached, then the dentist needs to suffer the consequences. Should he be killed? No. Should his family suffer death threats for his indiscretion? No. Should he be publically humiliated and should he lose his business? No. Should he pay a fine and maybe lose his hunting rights in Africa? Yes. This last scenario is a punishment that fits the violation, if there even was one. This last punishment is what a rational, well adjusted and mature individual would suggest.

During the firestorm, the internet was flooded with opinions, statements and commentaries on the tragic death of 'Cecil.' I often wonder who gave that vicious predator of Africa the name, Cecil. In my opinion, the naming of a wild animal is where the problem started.

I believe giving wild animals names is ridiculous. This of course is an extension of our domestication of animals for pets. Our dogs and cats have names, so why shouldn't wild animals? Simple, wild animals are wild, not domesticated by any means and want nothing to do with humans if they can help it. Do you think Cecil knew he was named? Do you think he came when he was called? The lion was wild, killed other animals and probably humans for food, and probably instilled nothing but unimaginable fear in the nearby villagers. Yet the anti-hunters here in America wanted justice for an animal that had lived its entire life in the wild; an animal they had never heard of before he was hunted. They likely never contributed a single penny to preserving lions or other animals, and are probably clueless when it comes to the natural history of the top predators of Africa.

Believe it or not this disconnection with a beloved animal that has only been encountered on television, is not only an attractive cause for the anti-hunter, it's desired. It provides the hands-off circumstances that allow them to distantly fight for without getting their supportive hands dirty. It's so simple to fight the internet fight from the comfort of their home. Petitions can be started, legislators can be contacted and individuals that think differently can be demeaned and attacked. Having no real connection to the cause means no real investment of time or money. This is the perfect storm of involvement for the anti-hunter.

Despite the killing of the lion, the money that the dentist spent for the opportunity to hunt in Zimbabwe did more for the lion population than the tens of thousands of individuals that jumped on the Cecil bandwagon that week and called for the dentist's head.

I would imagine that if the American people had to deal with African lions on a daily basis like the bush people of Zimbabwe, they'd feel far differently about the killing of one single lion so very far away.

While the media saturation of the story frothed up the anti-hunting culture in this country, an op-ed piece published in The New York Times in August 2015 presented a very unique perspective into the killing of a lion; a species that the author grew up living with and fearing in the same country where Cecil was killed.

In Zimbabwe, We Don't Cry for Lions
By Goodwell Nzou, Winston-Salem, N.C.

"My mind was absorbed by the biochemistry of gene editing when the text messages and Facebook posts distracted me.
'So sorry about Cecil.'
'Did Cecil live near your place in Zimbabwe?'
Cecil who? I wondered. When I turned on the news and discovered that the messages were about a lion killed by an American dentist, the village boy inside me instinctively cheered: One lion fewer to menace families like mine.

My excitement was doused when I realized that the lion killer was being painted as the villain. I faced the starkest cultural contradiction I'd experienced during my five years studying in the United States.

Did all those Americans signing petitions understand that lions actually kill people? That all the talk about Cecil being "beloved" or a "local favorite" was media hype? Did Jimmy Kimmel choke up because Cecil was killed or because he confused him with Simba from "The Lion King"?

In my village in Zimbabwe, surrounded by wildlife conservation areas, no lion has ever been beloved, or granted an affectionate nickname. They are objects of terror.

When I was 9 years old, a solitary lion prowled villages near my home. After it killed a few chickens, some goats and finally a cow, we were warned to walk to school in groups and stop playing

155

outside. *My sisters no longer went alone to the river to collect water or wash dishes; my mother waited for my father and older brothers, armed with machetes, axes and spears, to escort her into the bush to collect firewood.*

A week later, my mother gathered me with nine of my siblings to explain that her uncle had been attacked but escaped with nothing more than an injured leg. The lion sucked the life out of the village: No one socialized by the fires at night; no one dared stroll over to neighbor's homestead.

When the lion was finally killed, no one cared whether its killer was a local person or a white trophy hunter, whether it was poached or killed legally. We danced and sang about the vanquishing of the fearsome beast and our escape from serious harm.

Recently, a 14-year-old boy in a village not far from mine wasn't so lucky. Sleeping in his family's fields, as villagers do to protect crops from hippos, buffalo and elephants that trample them, he was mauled by a lion and died.

The killing of Cecil hasn't garnered much more sympathy from urban Zimbabweans, although they live with no such danger. Few have ever seen a lion, since game drives are a luxury residents of a country with an average monthly income below $150 cannot afford.

Don't misunderstand me: For Zimbabweans, wild animals have near-mystical significance. We belong to clans, and each clan claims an animal totem as its mythical ancestor. Mine is Nzou, elephant, and by tradition, I can't eat elephant meat; it would be akin to eating a relative's flesh. But our respect for these animals has never kept us from hunting them or allowing them to be hunted. (I'm familiar with dangerous animals; I lost my right leg to a snake bite when I was 11).

The American tendency to romanticize animals that have been given actual names and to jump onto a hashtag train has turned an ordinary situation – there were 800 lions legally killed over a decade by well-heeled foreigners who shelled out serious money to prove their prowess – into what seems to my Zimbabwean eyes an absurdist circus.

PETA is calling for the hunter to be hanged. Zimbabwean politicians are accusing the United States of staging Cecil's killing as a "ploy" to make our country look bad. And Americans, who can't find Zimbabwe on a map, are applauding the nations demand for the extradition of the dentist, unaware that a baby elephant was reportedly slaughtered for our president's most recent birthday banquet.

We Zimbabweans are left shaking our heads, wondering why Americans care more about African animals than about African people.

Don't tell us what to do with our animals when you allowed your own mountain lions to be hunted to near extinction in the eastern United States. Don't bemoan the clear-cutting of our forests when you turned yours into concrete jungles.

And please, don't offer me condolences about Cecil unless you're also willing to offer condolences for villagers killed or left hungry by his brethren, by political violence, or by hunger."

Goodwell Nzou, is a doctoral student in molecular and cellular biosciences at Wake Forest University.

I have seen dozens of these anti-hunting/hunter confrontations played out in the media over the years. However, a handful of times these interactions have been directed towards me and my daughters, usually after we posted hunting photos on social media. It didn't matter how badly they wanted to respond, I've taught my daughters to take the high road when dealing with those that will not listen to reason or facts. Our response to these individuals is always the same. We block their access to our accounts and their ability to view our content, and we remove their comments.

When it comes to our hobbies, I don't believe anyone should hate anything. I've always believed that hate is so foreign to the human condition that it can't be considered normal. Hypertension and stress, both common conditions of an elevated aggression and the perceived mood of hate, are scientifically proven to shorten your life. It would stand to reason, that from an evolutionary standpoint, this type of emotion would be selected against if it negatively affects life span.

It's clear that when anti-hunters attack legal hunting, they do so with hate. I used to work for someone that would routinely state that he hated certain people. When he'd make the statement, I felt it was childish, ridiculous and shined a very dull light on his character.

Anyone that actively sets out to hate anything must be bitter, always angry and they certainly have a very limited or non-existent capacity for any type of joy.

As hunters, we tap into the primal adrenalin rush of pursuing wild game and there is seriously nothing like it. This feeling is one of the reasons we hunt. Now consider an individual that will never understand that joy and excitement.

To conclude, we as hunters are passionate about our heritage and secure in the ways in which we support it. We have science on our side and that can never be refuted. We invest time and money in habitat rehabilitation and creation, off season scouting and the resource. More importantly, we strive to pass on our hunting interest to the next generation. As long as we stay strong, stay involved and educate those that will listen to reason, our passion for what we do can never be doused.

The bottom line is that our natural resources are healthy and will remain that way for hunters and non-hunters because of sportsmen. This is how we differ so greatly from the anti-hunters. They may argue that they too are passionate about their 'cause.' However, I don't consider an occasional misguided release of hate an example of passion.

All animals die

When non-hunters see a cute bunny in a local park or get a brief glimpse of a coyote at the edge of suburbia, they probably feel that they're experiencing much of what nature has to offer. I don't believe they realize that they're only getting a very brief glimpse of that animal's total life. While it's natural to feel privileged and lucky to get a quick look at wild animals, unlike non-hunters, sportsmen understand that all these beautiful animals will eventually die. Death in nature in most cases is violent, unexpected and at times, prolonged.

A majority of the non-hunting public have no idea how violent the natural world is. They get a quick sighting of the beauty of nature and have no concept of what those animals go through daily. In a world where everything is trying to kill and eat everything else, every day is a struggle for survival in the wild world. This can be a tough concept for some to grasp when everyday survival is not something most humans in our country have to deal with.

Even further from the minds of non-hunters is what lies at the end for most wild animals. Wild animals do not have the luxury of dying of old age. They don't die in their sleep and life doesn't just seep from their old bodies. The end of their lives is violent, unexpected and at times, not quick. I've personally witnessed bobcat slowly suffocating quail, and coyotes literally pull jack rabbits apart. In these cases there was no account for how the prey suffered, and suffer they did.

Many individuals that don't spend much time in the outdoors have no real concept of most aspects of nature. They're quick to adore the cute part or the brief glimpse, but they can't and in some cases won't stomach the violent side of the wild world. Sportsmen understand what can happen in the wild. We've seen the miracle of wild animal birth and the adorable spring young that appear during our scouting trips. We've also seen stuff that would make non-sportsmen turn away in horror.

I think the big difference between the two groups is that sportsmen understand all aspects of nature, including the dark and ugly side. We've seen what some animals do to others, and how life in the outdoors is a daily struggle for survival. I've seen what's leftover of a fawn once coyotes get a hold of it, understanding that every second of that dismantling was done while the baby deer was alive. I've watched a red-tail hawk pick at the guts of a live baby rabbit as it screamed from the raptor's perch at the top of a telephone pole. I've seen two coyotes play tug-of-war with a live jack rabbit, finally ripping it apart after a full minute of suffering.

These events didn't change my view of the wild world. They simply served as reminders that life for wild animals is not always fuzzy, cuddly and suitable for a Hallmark card. As sportsmen, we are used to these types of episodes. We understand that nature is beautiful and violent.

I believe that the lack of exposure to the violent side of nature causes non-hunters to be confused and unfamiliar with the site of dead animals. I think it's that simple. I don't think they believe that animals ever die, and the idea of seeing a proud hunter standing over the animal they've killed confuses them and makes their responses irrational and emotional. It's almost like they treat nature sightings and the eventual death of an animal, as separate unrelated events. Almost like they believe that violent death is not a part of nature and they refuse to accept it. It is this disconnect that makes any argument they may have towards hunting and hunters unsubstantiated and weak. Just because they may be unfamiliar with a sequence of events, doesn't make it wrong.

Sportsmen are so in tune with all levels of the natural world that we are not repulsed by the sight of a dead animal that has been hunted. On the contrary, we feel respect and admiration. I personally approach any downed animal with the same two emotions; a small bit of sadness, and an immense amount of gratitude. I'm immensely humbled at the sacrifice that will fill my freezer. I also fully understand that if I hadn't killed the animal to feed my family, it would've met its demise in a far more violent and prolonged manner in the natural world.

Respecting our history

I've always had great respect and admiration for those that laid the ground work for any movement. I consider these individuals pioneers, those that existed in a time before modern conveniences, and those that through hard work, dedication and survival necessity, figured out how to get things done. It doesn't matter what activity you discuss or are interested in, someone was involved in it before you were, and assisted in making it better and easier. For this reason, these individuals deserve our respect.

We should feel no different about those that hunted before us; long before us. Every human that has existed and will exist should respect those that made man the top predator on the planet. It doesn't matter if you hunt or not, our place as a species is a result of man hunting and eating meat. Plant eaters don't rule the world, meat eaters do!

It has been well established that the presence of modern man on the planet dates back to about 35,000 to 40,000 years ago. During this time, Homo sapiens moved into northeastern Siberia. This group of nomadic humans was skilled hunters, using crude tools to kill and butcher game. Some of these individuals migrated into North America via the Bering Plain about 15,000 to 20,000 years ago. This time period marks the evolution of more specialized tools for processing hunted game into food, a transition from nomadic hunting and gathering lifestyle to agriculture and settlement, and ultimately civilization. Beginning in Siberia, if we consider this time period as the true beginning of modern man's pursuit of game for food, and we can, man has been an established hunter in his modern form for at least 40,000 years.

This means that modern man has been hunting and gathering on this planet for thousands of generations. As a species, we have been hunting our own protein and killing our own food for a very long time.

In relative recent history we have developed technologies that have brought modernization and convenience to our food acquisition and preservation. The biggest advancement is the development of home freezers and refrigeration units.

In 1805, an American inventor named Oliver Evans designed the first refrigeration machine. Based on Evan's principles, American physician John Gorrie built a refrigerator in 1844 to cool his patients. Commercial fridge and freezer units were in use for almost 40-years prior to the introduction of home models. Practical household refrigerators were introduced in 1915 and gained wider acceptance in the United States in the 1930's as prices fell. This means in modern human history, the ability for the general public to keep food cold, frozen and preserved longer with the use of home refrigeration units is less than 100-years old, or less than two generations.

With this relatively new refrigeration technology, modern man has been able obtain their protein from refrigerated markets, and out of convenience, have become less dependent on killing their own meat for food. Neatly packaged protein was available at the local butcher's shop or carefully carved, packaged and labeled at your local market. Unfortunately, this convenience has spawned a mindset that since we no longer need to hunt for our food that hunting was and is bad.

Modern man has honed his hunting skills for literally thousands of generations, obtaining meat for his tribe to live and thrive on. From the dawn of man until less than a hundred years ago, hunting was as common and acceptable as walking. Now, in less than a generation, a segment of society, those that have likely never actively hunted for their own food, have not only turned their backs on the activity of hunting, they have actively condemned it.

How can a portion of the current generation so despise an activity that has not only sustained us as a people in our current form the entire time we've been on the planet, but dismiss it without every participating in it?

To me this illustrates a narrow view of our history and a lack of empathy for those who suffered through the life and death struggle of pre-civilization. These individuals live in the now and have no thought, compassion or concept of how, we as humans, have developed and evolved. Our teeth tell the story. We have eaten meat since the beginning, and up until about 100 years ago, it was completely acceptable and necessary for us to chase it down and kill it ourselves.

Since these narrow-minded individuals have decide to elevate themselves above the so-called primal and brutal concept of hunting our own protein and completely disregard those that laid the nutritional path before them, I think it's absolutely fair to reduce the general populace into a few simple categories. The way I see it, there are three types of people on the planet; hunters, vegans and hypocrites. I categorize hunters as those that hunt and those that don't, but support the activity, vegans as those that choose to consume non-animal protein and plant matter, and those hypocritical individuals that constantly condemn hunting while holding a drumstick.

When it comes to legal activities, I don't believe anyone should be anti anything. If you dislike an activity, you should mind your own business and stay quiet. I don't like ballet or watch bull fighting, but I certainly don't spend my spare time denouncing either activity, or picketing on Broadway. When it comes to our hobbies, passions or activities, I have a very dim view of those that argue against something they know very little about, especially an activity that is so entrained in our culture.

If you eat meat, and voice negativity towards hunting, you are a hypocrite. If you wear leather, or possess anything made of leather, or wear anything made of fur and denounce hunting, you need to stop making yourself look foolish and either educate yourself or stay silent. Above all, whether you like hunting or not, you need to understand its role in human history and respect it.

Should we all stick together?

One of the reasons I enjoy hunting so much is that the activity itself is so diverse. Sportsmen have so many options in what type of game they wish to chase, how they wish to hunt and where they decide to travel. Add in the dozens of different weapons that can be used to hunt from archery, to muzzle loader, to air gun, to spear, to shotgun, to center fire, to crossbow, and the combinations and individual interests are almost endless.

Unfortunately, at times, it's this diversity that tends to divide our hunting ranks. For whatever reason, some hunters like to deem one type of hunting better or more preferred than others. So much so, that they look down or degrade the legal methods by which others hunt.

I'm of the opinion that all sportsmen in general should support other sportsmen no matter what method they choose to legally hunt, and whatever legal game they choose to chase. In the legal pursuit of game, we are a brotherhood and we need to embrace our diversity and tolerate the differences. I believe we need to step back and learn from those differences. Whether we participate in a particular type of hunting or not, we need to stand shoulder to shoulder with all ethical sportsmen and support them. We are all chasing one desire and one dream.

The obvious exception to this ideology is when a sportsman breaks the rules. I absolutely refuse to extend this umbrella of brotherhood to those individuals that choose to ignore the game laws. I believe the outdoor community need to voice our displeasure loudly when one of our own, poaches, hunts on protected land or does something stupid that makes us all look bad.

Part of being a hunter is following a self-imposed code of ethics and we need to strongly advertise this. The segment of the hunting community that gives hunters a bad name will almost always garner the most attention by the non-hunting public. These are the individuals that will eventually show up on the evening news for all the wrong reasons.

Each one of us is an ambassador for our hunting heritage. Whenever we're in the field or involved in anything outdoors, it's our job to act in our own best interest. We need to demonstrate that we are responsible stewards of the resource and lead by example. Integrity and character are measured when no one's looking, and we need to show that to other hunters and non-hunters alike. Be friendly, be humble, clean up after yourselves and show the animals the respect they deserve.

What we do as hunters is important, it's legal and it's our heritage. We as outdoorsmen and women understand how important hunting is to resource management, and preserving game species health and populations for future generations. Don't ever apologize for being a hunter, feel like you have to justify your interest in hunting or feel like you need to hide your hunting identity. Wear your camo with pride and always look to educate the uninformed.

For the most part I do believe that all sportsmen need to support each other and stick together. Hunting is much more than a passion for most sportsmen, it's a lifestyle. Just like with any other popular activity, you don't have to support everyone that participates, but you should at least strongly support the cause.

Pig vs. Pig

From 1909 to 2012, the USDA reported that beef, pork and chicken were the most popular meats consumed by Americans in that 100-year period. I think it's safe to assume this trend will continue into the unforeseen future, especially for non-sportsmen and non-hunters.

Examining this group of domesticated and mass produced animals, we can conclude that two of the three creatures do not have any true surrogates or similar species in the wild. In this country, we don't actively hunt cows or chickens, and most Americans have become used to seeing these animals represented in only one way; cut up and package at the back of the supermarket. However, the same cannot be said for the pig.

Currently, wild hogs can be found in three quarters of the U.S. states and the U.S. Department of Agriculture estimates the population to be in the neighborhood of 5 million nationwide. Their expanding range has made them one of the most popular big game animals pursued by hunters. They are fast, smart and tough to bring down. The first big game animal I ever killed was a wild pig, and I still find them a challenge to chase.

The pork that is found in supermarkets does not come from wild hogs. Those pigs are raised specifically for human consumption on large pig farms that can mass produce thousands of animals a month. These pigs are not wild by any means, and would be about as challenging to hunt as hitting a pillow with a bat.

All sportsmen know the difference between the wild hogs that run the hills, and the ones that are raised in the dark and stand in their own filth. With a domesticated and wild representative member of the species on each side of the pork fence, we are afforded a unique opportunity to compare the lives of each animal.

Physically, there are some significant differences among the two types. Mass produced pigs have shorter noses, floppy ears, and curly tails. They have shorter legs and are almost hairless. In contrast, wild hogs have thicker, bristlier coats, a noticeable ridge of hair running along their backs, longer, straighter tails, and longer legs and head.

Domesticated pigs raised in mass, spend their entire lives inside. Breeding sows are kept in pens so narrow they are unable to turn around. They are fed constantly and administered low-level antibiotics to prevent sickness. They are artificially inseminated and kept in the pens until they give birth. The air they breathe is stifled with the stench of ammonia and hydrogen sulfide generated from the abundance of pig waste accumulating below the pig holding area. These gases are poisonous and are ever present throughout the life of the pig.

Once the piglets arrive, the sow is removed from the gestation crate and spends 2-3 weeks nursing the litter. After this period, the piglets are removed from the sow before they're weaned and she is placed back in the crate, where she is once again artificially inseminated. She will repeat this process throughout her life, until she is no longer healthy enough to reproduce. At that time, she will be slaughtered and processed for consumption, having spent her entire life in a gestation crate.

The piglets are separated by sex. Males are castrated to avoid issues with excess testosterone tainting the flavor of the meat. This is done without any anesthetic to avoid meat contamination. Both sexes have their tails cut off to discourage tail biting, a common crowding behavior among domestic swine. Again, this is done without any sedative or numbing agent.

The young pigs are place in larger pens with other pigs and fed a mixture of grain and protein (meat and bone meal) to fatten them up. Depending on the market, these young pigs can be slaughtered anywhere from the piglet stage on up. The pigs that are processed for human consumption are slaughtered at around six months of age. It is suggested that approximately 100 million pigs are produced annually in this fashion here in the United States. This is where your pork chops and bacon comes from.

Wild pigs are born in the wild. When conditions are favorable, they can breed year round. A healthy sow will have 1-2 litters a year and during optimum conditions, she can produce up to a dozen piglets per litter. However, it is more likely that average litters are about 5-6 piglets in size. During their first month of life they are very vulnerable to predators. Coyotes, bobcats and mountain lions will prey on the young until they are big enough to defend themselves. Mountain lions will occasionally take a larger animal, but traveling in larger family groups assists in keeping the pigs safe.

Sows are reproductively active as young as six months, but probably don't start breeding until after their first year. Males will stay with the family group until they become too aggressive or are kicked out by stronger males. Lone boars will remain solitary or form bachelor groups and travel together.

Piglets will stay with their mother until they are weaned. They'll then begin feeding on plant material and remain with the family group their entire lives. Wild pigs are opportunistic omnivores, meaning they eat just about anything. Approximately 80-90% of their diet consists of plant matter, like grasses, roots and anything they can dig up. The remainder of their diet consists of animal protein.

Staying in large family groups allows for increased threat detection. They'll often sleep in large pig piles, lying on top of each other to conserve warmth.

With their elongated noses, wild pigs have an amazing sense of smell, and rely on that and exceptional hearing to protect them from predators. Their eyesight is not great, but they are by no means blind. They can easily pick up movement at a distance, and then use their other acute senses to identify the threat.

Here in California, large boars can reach 300-pounds, with large sows tipping the scales at between 200-250 pounds. Wild pigs have a lifespan of between 4 and 8 years of age, and once they reach adulthood, their only consistent threat is man.

Wild pigs are challenging to hunt. Their meat is lean and delicious, and I personally prefer it over store-bought pork. They are completely wild and are born, live and die never knowing the confines of a pen or a windowless barn. They root, wallow and feed at will. No part of a true wild pig's life is manipulated by man.

Mass produced pigs never feel grass under their feet or feel the warmth of the sun. They spend their entire, short lives inside, crowded and force fed. Every single step of their lives is manipulated so that a consistent supply of pork parts can be beautifully arranged and packaged at the back of the supermarket for our convenience.

So, knowing what we know now about these two forms of pig, I ask you one simple question; which pig has the better life, the domesticated animal that will never feel grass beneath its feet or be warmed by the sun, or the wild pig that spent every second of its life outside, free and whose life may end suddenly and unexpectedly by a hunter in the wild? If I were a pig, I know where I'd rather be.

Sportsmen's contribution

Most sportsmen and women understand how much we contribute to the natural resource through our actions, our purchases of outdoor gear and our dedication to conservation programs. The National Shooting Sports Foundation has created a handy HunterFactCard that outlines the specifics of exactly what sportsmen contribute to the resource.

Sportsmen contribute nearly $8 million every day to resource conservation, for a total of $2.9 billion annually. Through the Pittman-Robertson Act established in 1937, hunters and target shooters have contributed $7.1 billion in the form of excise taxes on outdoor gear.

Hunting and hunting related activities is big business, generating 600,000 jobs nationwide. In more than 80-years, sportsmen have paid more than $14 billion for habitat restoration and on-the-ground projects in every state, protecting our natural environment and our fish and wildlife.

Coupled with the immense monetary contributions, the recovery numbers over the last hundred years or so of some of the more popular game species is a true testament of how much, we as sportsmen continue to do for the resource. It's important to note that these recovery numbers are sustained and consistent because sportsmen assign value to the resource and continue to use science to maintain these optimum population levels.

In 1900, there were less than half a million white-tailed deer remaining in the nation. Through conservation programs and resource education, the Quality Deer Management Association reported in 2013 that the current count was now 32,000,000.

In 1901, there was no accurate count for ducks and waterfowl, but the population was determined to be extremely low. The USFWS report that the 2013 count was 46,000,000.

A 1907 elk count by the National Parks Service determined that only 41,000 elk remained in the United States. A 2013 census showed that the population breached the one million mark, and that elk were now thriving in 23 states.

Many have no idea how close the wild turkey came to complete nationwide extinction. A count in the early 1900's tallied only 100,000 birds. Encroaching civilization and habitat loss contributed to the decline. Dedicated turkey groups and conservation programs have increased the nationwide population to 7,000,000.

About 50-years ago, the total U.S. population of pronghorn was only about 12,000. Today, with conservation programs and resource education, in 2011 Texas Parks and Wildlife reported the population has increased to over 1,100,000.

These recovery numbers are even more impressive when you think that not only were these animals actively hunted during this period, but the human population in this country in 1900 was 76,000,000, a fraction of the 320,000,000 it is now.

These numbers do not lie. Sportsmen are directly responsible for the health and wellbeing of this countries game species, and we have been for over 100-years. We contribute time and money to the cause, and through habitat restoration, benefit non-game species as well. Our outdoor passion is reflected in the game species recovery numbers and continues today. Wild animals, both game and non-game species are healthy, sustainable and present for hunters and non-hunters to enjoy because of the contributions of sportsmen. The next time someone asks why you hunt, tell them that it's so that everyone, even non-hunters can enjoy our natural resources.

TIME TO HUNT

Much like when they first started shooting with me, there were successes and failures when Jessica and Alyssa started actively hunting with me. When we encountered frustrating issues, mistakes or misses, we handled them just like we had when they were learning to shoot; if they were unhappy with their performance, I told them they needed to practice to get better. I have never been one to coddle my kids and I don't subscribe to the notion that everyone should get a trophy. In fact, I believe the notion of rewarding all achievements, good and mediocre, is the worst form of reinforcement.

Conversely, when they did well, I let them know how proud I was of them, making sure they realized how far they've come. Once they experienced some hunting successes, and they started putting all they've learned to use, they got noticeably better. My reward was that I got to watch them become hunters.

Since there was a considerable stagger in years and interest between my daughters during this process, it stands to reason that they would enter the hunting level differently, and they did. Alyssa was ready from day one, and seemed to countdown the days until she was old enough to take the hunter's safety course and get her license. Jessica's interest seemed to blossom near the age of ten, when she started to see Alyssa's hunting successes. Much like the early target training, Alyssa eased into hunting at an early level and Jessica just jumped in when she was mature enough to decide for herself that she was ready.

Once they acquired their hunting licenses and were ready to head out to the field, my initial approach was to introduce them to the types of hunting that offered increased shot opportunities and plentiful game, thus a higher possibility of success. I knew that my love for other types of hunting may influence the order by which they entered the hunting guild, but I decided to start them off where I had started; small game hunting.

The day after Alyssa passed her Hunter's Safety course here in California, we went out to pick up her very first hunting license. I had known for some time that Alyssa really wanted to start hunting with me, but I didn't understand just how much until we went to get her first license.

Here in California, young hunters can hunt upland game for free and don't have to buy an upland game bird stamp. When we went to get Alyssa's license, there seemed to be some confusion about this as the cashier wrung up our fees. After a brief discussion on the regulations, the cashier realized her mistake, adjusted the cost and printed out the license minus the upland stamp. When I handed it to Alyssa she had tears in her eyes. She thought that without an upland stamp she wouldn't be allowed to hunt upland game. After I explained the regulations for junior hunters to her, she smiled and instantly started asking when I could take her on her first hunt as a licensed hunter.

Alyssa's first animal

Four days after getting her license, Alyssa and I were out in the desert shooting targets. She made it clear that after the target practice, she wanted to drive around looking for jack rabbits. The surrounding area was home to both cottontail rabbits and jacks, but she knew the jack rabbits were larger, and just like my very first game animal, Alyssa wanted to chase the jack.

Despite having her own pink Cricket, single-shot .22, Alyssa had been spending a lot more time practicing with my Ruger 10/22 semi-automatic rifle. She was used to loading it, aiming and shooting it, and she was deadly accurate with that firearm. The Ruger was the rifle she had chosen for her very first hunt.

Once we were done with target practice, I put the unloaded rifle in the back seat. I handed Alyssa two loaded clips and we headed out to look for jack rabbits. We slowly drove around the rugged desert roads for about an hour looking for game. Alyssa was very excited and used her binoculars to search through the open window. It wasn't unusually for us to spot jacks sitting in the shade of bushes, waiting out the midday sun.

We rounded a corner and a large jack raced across the road about 75-yards in front us. The rabbit dropped into a dry creek bed and started running up a canyon on the left side of the dirt two-track. Within seconds of spotting him, he was out of sight. I pulled off the road and grabbed the rifle. Alyssa grabbed her shooting sticks and the clips and we started hiking the adjacent ridge. As soon as we crested the slight mound above the creek, I spotted the jack resting in the shade of a large bush about 75-yards away.

I loaded the .22 as Alyssa sat down in the dirt and adjusted her sticks. I carefully put the rifle on her shooting sticks and pointed out the jack. Alyssa got comfortable and adjusted the set up a bit. She found the resting jack in the scope and got ready. After a calming breath, she squeezed the trigger on her first hunted animal.

At the shot, the rabbit jumped a few feet and then fell over dead. Alyssa, at the age of ten, had her first animal as a licensed hunter; the same species that had started my hunting journey 35-years earlier.

We walked over to the rabbit and both of us knelt down next to it. I wanted Alyssa to understand the importance of what she had just done. During her target training, I explained to her that once she fires a weapon, there is no taking that bullet back. The bullet can't be stopped until it hits whatever it's aimed at. There, at the site of her first kill, I reminded her that she had pulled the trigger to end this animal's life and with every hunted animal, there is some sadness that a hunter experiences. We talked about how this was completely normal, and I told her that I still feel a moment of finality with every animal I kill. I didn't want take away from her excitement, but I wanted her to understand the seriousness of the event.

She looked at me, smiled and nodded her head slowly. She looked back down at the rabbit and I knew nothing else needed to be said. She gently grabbed the back legs of the jack and picked it up. "I'm eating this thing tonight," she said. As we walked to the truck, I knew that, much like me, my daughter Alyssa had been born a hunter.

Later that evening I cooked up the jack and together we ate Alyssa's first hunted animal. After years of meeting me at the back of the truck and years of dedicated target practice, my daughter had hunted in the wild and brought home game for our family. Sitting there with Alyssa over a paper plate of fried jack rabbit that she had killed, I realized that the hunting circle was now complete.

In the months that followed, Alyssa added several more rabbits to her tally. It got to the point that if she spotted a rabbit within range, it didn't stand a chance. As soon as she figured out the jack rabbits, I knew what species she wanted to chase next.

Alyssa with her first hunted animal. Just like I had, Alyssa entered the hunter's fold by shooting a jack rabbit. Once she acquired her hunting license, there was no stopping her (Hovey 2010).

Alyssa's first coyote

Before Alyssa had her hunting license, almost all of her early hunts were predator hunts. She would sit beside me as an observer as I called, searching the terrain like a pro. She was an absolute statue during those hunts, and from an early age she seemed to understand that being still was paramount to success. She became intrigued with the stealthy nature of the predator calling game and whenever we were out, that's what she wanted to do.

She was safe beyond words and handled every firearm with the focus of someone well beyond her years. With her California junior hunting license in hand and close to five years of practice, I felt she was ready to be the shooter on a predator hunting stand in 2012.

We planned a Sunday trip in early October. Alyssa had been getting some trigger time with the Ruger .204 and the 22-250 during our target sessions. She had easily gotten used to the larger calibers and shot them both very well.

On a previous predator stand with her on the rifle, I called in a coyote that came in fast. Alyssa spotted the huge male and moved her set up to get into position. Unfortunately, the approaching coyote spotted her movement and left quickly without offering her a shot. I remember looking over at her and smiling. "He saw me move, didn't he?" she asked. I just nodded and continued to smile. A lesson learned.

We arrived at the hunting area in the early afternoon. After some searching and a few blank stands, I found an amazing spot towards the end of the day. We set up quietly overlooking a shallow drainage that ran from our left to right. The perfect terrain stretched out in front of us for over a mile. The sun had dipped behind the hills and from our perch we could see anything that approached. I set Alyssa up on her sticks, rifle pointing right, towards the upstream portion of the dry creek. I sat behind her and a little to her left. She reached up and clicked on her noise-dampening ear muffs and pulled up her face mask. I asked if she heard me in a whisper and she nodded. It was time to get started.

I started calling and searching. I could see Alyssa slowly moving her head looking for movement of any kind in the brush. I smiled as I knew she had already applied what she had learned from her last coyote encounter. She was becoming a hunter.

After about twelve minutes Alyssa slowly held out her hand, extending all five fingers. This was our code for "how much longer?" The area looked too good to leave, and with the expanse of land in front of us, I wanted to give it more time. I knew it was going to be our last stand of the day and I decided we'd just stay put and continue calling. I held up three fingers indicating three more minutes. It's a good thing that I did.

The coyote came trotting in way to our left at about the fifteen minute mark and if I hadn't been looking that way when he popped out of the drainage, I never would've spotted him. I whispered to Alyssa that we had a coyote coming and her head whipped around fast. I told her to calm down and to move slowly. Truth be told, I was a wreck inside. It was difficult to maintain my own composure and let Alyssa run the stand, but that's exactly what I did. I could hear her excited breathing as she spotted the coyote weaving its way through the thick cover. With her rifle pointing way right, she needed to move it at least 120-degrees to the left to have a chance. I saw her wiggle in her seat slightly, preparing to make the move when the coyote wasn't looking.

When the approaching predator dropped behind some brush, I whispered to move on him. Alyssa quickly and quietly lifted her set up and rotated into position as the coyote peaked out and stopped. His behavior clearly illustrated that he had no idea we were there. He looked around, tested the wind, and looked over his shoulder and then right back at us. I whispered don't move. He stared right through us for a full minute and then looked out towards the mountains. Alyssa moved her rifle a bit more. I asked her if she's was on him. She didn't answer me. "Can you see him in the scope?" I whispered. No answer. The shot surprised me and I heard it smack the coyote. He spun twice and then tipped over in the brush about 95-yards from where we were sitting. Alyssa worked the bolt on the rifle and her excited breath escaped her all at once in a very shaky tone. "DADDY, I GOT HIM, I GOT HIM!"

I was speechless. I could feel tears welling up in my eyes as I hugged her. She was shaking with excitement. I seriously couldn't believe it. I knew that she would have many chances during her first season to shoot a coyote, but I had no idea she would be successful at the beginning of her first season as a licensed hunter.

I made the rifle safe and we walked down to the animal and knelt next to it. She petted the fur and I explained to her that even though I love hunting coyotes, I have a tremendous amount of respect for them. We sat there in silence for a moment and I grabbed its back legs to carry it back to the truck. "No daddy, I want to carry him" she said. She struggled with the thirty pound animal, but eventually made it back to the truck, carrying it by herself.

I've shot a lot of coyotes over the years, but I have never been more nervous and excited as I was on that stand. Watching Alyssa seamlessly slip into hunt mode that day and embrace a seriousness that was well beyond her years was impressive. I often think back to that hunt and how it unfolded, and I can't think of anything she could've improved on. That day and that stand are a special memory both of us will keep for the rest of our lives. As a dad, I couldn't have been prouder. As the hunts piled up and she gathered more experience, Alyssa only got better.

Alyssa with her first coyote. Her familiarity with her gear and her training enabled her to capitalize on her first predator opportunity. I believe, much like me, Alyssa was born a hunter (Hovey 2012).

Alyssa's first bobcat

Once Alyssa had her license, it was pretty much a given that when I went hunting, she went with me. With her early success and her increasing interest, hunting quickly became her new passion. Even when we weren't out chasing game, she'd ask all sorts of questions about hunting and when we were headed out again. After she shot her first coyote, all she wanted to do was hunt predators.

A few weeks after Alyssa shot her first coyote, we headed out to hunt predators again. The night before the trip, we stopped off and picked up her very first bobcat tag. With the early stages of a severe drought gripping California, the predator hunting in and around our hunting area had been poor. During the 2012 season I had only seen a handful of coyotes and only one bobcat. That apparently didn't matter to Alyssa. She had a license, it was early in the bobcat season and if we were headed out to call predators, she wanted a tag.

We got an early start and began the day with some target practice. At around noon we had lunch on the tailgate and discussed a plan for the hunt. We ate quickly, changed into some camo and headed out to do some calling.

On the last stand of the day, we set up overlooking a dry drainage with the setting sun at our backs. Off to our right was one of the only running desert springs near the dry creek. When Alyssa heard I had called and killed a bobcat the year before at the desert spring stand, she wanted to make sure we called there before the day ended.

We got our rifles set up and started calling. The wounded bird sound echoed off the opposite canyon and filled the drainage. Alyssa searched the left side and I searched the right. At the two-minute mark we had a hard charging coyote come in from my side and stop broadside out at 60-yards. Alyssa spotted him before he stopped and quickly got him in her sights. The coyote was stone still when she took the shot. Unfortunately, the light 204 bullet hit some brush and deflected before it hit the target.

The coyote took off and stopped out at 125-yards. I got him in the crosshairs and dropped him there. Alyssa was pretty disappointed at the miss, but she kept her composure and reloaded. Since it was early in the stand, we decided to keep calling.

A few minutes later Alyssa spotted another animal coming in fast from our right. "Coyote!" she whispered, simultaneously moving her set up to intercept the animal. I spotted the predator and realized it wasn't a coyote, but a large bobcat coming in quickly, running down the same path the coyote had used minutes earlier.

I leaned over and told Alyssa that the animal was a bobcat and she got very excited. The cat had raced at full speed down the creek until it got to the bank below us where we lost sight of it. I knew the bobcat was now in stealth mode and may be tough to spot in the thick vegetation. Cats don't just run in haphazardly or carelessly like some coyotes. Once they identify where the prey may be located, they sneak in silently.

Almost a minute passed before we spotted the bobcat again. He had covered almost twenty yards undetected and was now only ten feet from the call and about 40-yards from us. Before I could point him out, Alyssa spotted the cat and moved her set up over quietly. The bobcat would appear briefly in small gaps in the vegetation as he slowly belly-crawled towards the caller. I could see Alyssa slowly following him in the scope, waiting for a clear shot. "Take the shot if you have it" I whispered. Less than a second later, the crack of Alyssa's rifle was punctuated by a puff of fur and the cat dropped from view.

I made both rifles safe quickly and I ran down to where we had last seen the cat. I found the tuft of fur laying only three feet from the caller, but the bobcat was not there. I took three steps and found the dead bobcat lying below a small dirt mound. Alyssa's shot was perfect. I couldn't believe it. Her second trip out and I found myself filling out her very first bobcat tag; a tag we had purchased only nineteen hours earlier.

We collected her prize and took dozens of photos. We ended up taking two coyotes and Alyssa's bobcat on that short hunt and to this day, the photos of that hunt are some of my favorite.

I skinned the cat and carefully cut the back straps off the animal. On the drive out, I had told Alyssa that back in the day, many old trappers would eat the bobcats that they took. As soon as the cat hit the dirt, she made it clear that we were cooking bobcat for dinner.

Those first hunts marked Alyssa's introduction into the hunting world. Her early success with predators, a type of hunting I consider difficult to master, boosted her confidence towards other types of hunting. Once she began to experience some success and she started to apply all she had learned, her number one goal was to be the best hunter she could be.

Alyssa's first bobcat was almost as big as she was. This was her first trip out after cats and her bobcat tag was only nineteen hours old when we pinned it on this animal (Hovey 2012).

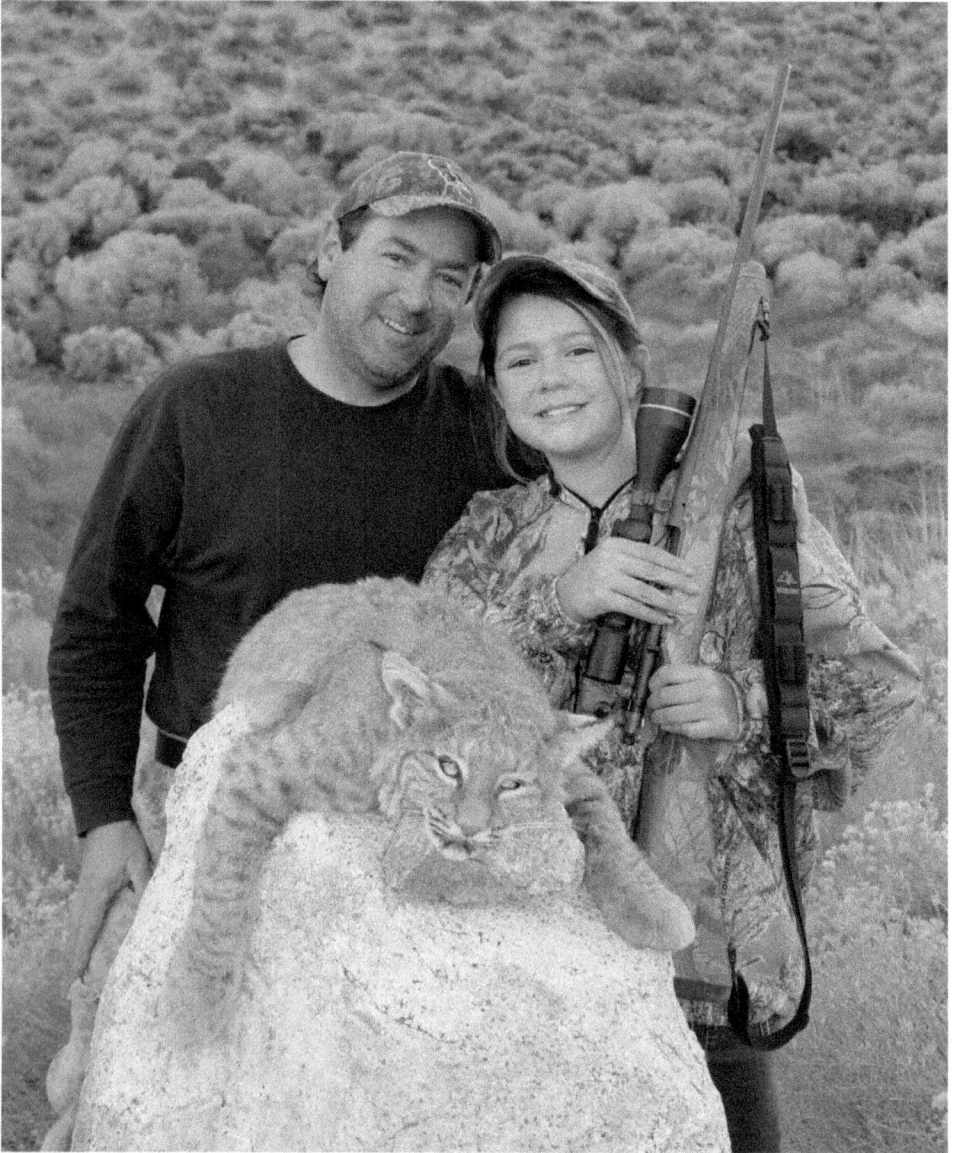

Alyssa and the Ruger .204 are a deadly combination (Hovey 2012).

The end of special treatment

Going into Alyssa's third year as a hunter, she was eager to start hunting again. While she was interested in adding new species to her hunting list, she really wanted to start the season off by chasing the animals where she began her hunting journey. She wanted to set aside some time to call predators again.

Alyssa had already shot a couple of coyotes by the time her third season rolled around and she had tagged her first bobcat at the beginning of her second year as a hunter. These early successes were the result of me setting her up and letting her be the shooter on over a dozen calling stands. During each instance, I held the shot on the animal to let her take the predator because that is what we were there to do. When we started our third calling season, I told her I was moving her up from trainee to team member. In other words, things would be different.

In early 2015 Alyssa and I set out for an all day predator hunt. I had scouted some new spots and I was anxious to call the area. After a few blank stands, Alyssa got a brief taste of the new arrangement. We had set up sitting next to each other and facing the same direction. The caller was out about 50-yards and we were ten minutes into the stand, when we got surprised.

A coyote crossed in front of us at a trot. He had come in on Alyssa's side and she was following him with the 204, waiting for him to stop. I caught him late, but tried to put the crosshairs on him before he disappeared on the other side of the stand. I found him in the scope and squeezed off a quick shot, but rushed it and missed. The coyote was gone before she could pull the trigger. She didn't say anything, but I could tell that she was a bit puzzled on why I had taken a shot without waiting for her. On the very next stand, she would be introduced to her place on Team Hovey.

Alyssa was covering the left side and I was covering the right. The caller and a Mojo decoy were set out about 50-yards directly in front of us. The caller had been running at full volume for a little less than five minutes when I caught movement out in front of us. When I spotted him, the coyote was trotting away leaving. I moved my sticks over and found him in the scope. As I did, I heard Alyssa move her set up, as she had spotted the coyote as well. Half a second later the coyote stopped and I squeezed off a shot with the 22-250 and dropped him at about 125-yards. Alyssa was not happy.

"Daddy, I had him in the scope!" she snapped. I played it off, saying that I didn't want another one getting away. She seemed to think that she deserved the first try at the coyote mainly because that's the way we had hunted before. I explained that now that she was hunting with me, we were a team and whoever could connect with the animal safely first was cleared for the shot. While she seemed to understand, she was still a bit angry.

My point here is that when we start teaching our kids how to hunt, we make sure that we do all we can for them so they'll be successful. After they achieve that success, I believe it's important that they know their continued success will take dedication on their part. I decided to explain the new arrangement to Alyssa at the beginning of her third hunting season. After a few hunts, she began to understand her place on the team and actually became a better hunter. She became more confident in her abilities, understood she was responsible for her own gear and that her special treatment was over. I think strongly that after initial success, in order to get better and strive for their next hunting level, they need to experience trial and failure. I'm not saying to stop guiding them; I'm just saying that challenging them a little bit is healthy and helpful.

Alyssa graduating from special treatment. Once she understood that making it to Team Hovey would ultimately make her a better hunter, she embraced her new role (Hovey 2015).

The awakening of Jessica

To this day, I don't think I could identify the reason why Jessica suddenly decided she wanted to hunt. She had been shooting and shooting well for several years, but I could tell the hunting interest wasn't quite there. I don't think it was fear or apprehension; I just think she wanted to decide for herself when she was ready.

Prior to every trip, I would ask Jessica if she wanted to head out with me, but she would always politely decline. When her sister started to become successful as a young hunter, I did notice Jessica perk up a bit. She seemed interested to hear how our hunting trips had gone, but actually participating wouldn't come until she was a little older.

A month or two before her tenth birthday, Jessica decided that she wanted to move beyond just shooting. I was headed out on a quick predator hunt after work and she asked if she could go. During that single stand hunt, we had an amazing encounter with a very small bobcat that neither one of us will ever forget. On the trip home, Jessica asked me if I could sign her up to take the hunter's safety course so she could get her hunting license. Jessica was ready to start hunting.

Jessica's first hunt

In 2013 I decided to start taking dedicated solo hunts with Alyssa once a year. Her passion to chase critters was intoxicating and I wanted to nurture her interest as much as possible. We would head out towards our hunting area, hunting in the evening, spend the night in a desert town nearby and then hunt our way home.

A few months after our first father/daughter trip, Jessica told me that she wanted in on the fun. She had scored a near perfect score on her safety test and was ready to move beyond targets. Once she conquered some early shooting apprehension and self-corrected her eye dominance issue, one thing became very clear to me; Jessica was an amazing shot. I knew if I could put an animal in front of her, she would take care of the rest.

My plan to start her on small game, like I had done with her older sister, was quickly rejected by Jessica. Her early exposure to predator hunting had planted the seed of interest. I'm sure seeing Alyssa's early predator hunting success had a lot to do with her desire to jump straight to hunting coyotes. Prior to her first hunt, Jessica had only sat on one predator stand with me and she had never seen a coyote come racing into the call. At the time of our first hunt, predator numbers were way down due to the drought and we were calling late in the season. I was not at all optimistic about success.

None of that mattered to Jessica. Despite her lack of experience hunting predators, she really wanted to kill a coyote.

The day after she passed her hunter's safety test, we purchased her very first California junior hunting license. Before we even made it to the parking lot, she asked, "So daddy, when are we going hunting?"

In January of 2014 Jessica and I headed out for our first father/daughter, overnight hunting trip. The plan was to hunt some of my favorite stands very near where we'd be staying the night. The following morning, we'd grab a hearty breakfast and then start hunting our way home. While I wasn't terribly optimistic about our chances, it was great to have this time with my youngest daughter. Besides, Jessica was so enthusiastic to get out that it really didn't matter how the hunt unfolded.

On the last stand of day one, we set up overlooking a flat area near a marsh. We were running out of daylight, so I set up quickly and started calling. Jessica sat like a statue, searching the area for movement. With the fading daylight, I knew this was going to be the last stand of the day.

At the ten-minute mark, we had a cautious coyote sneak in to about 100-yards of where we were set up. I caught him coming in, but lost sight of him in the thick cover. After that, I never saw him again. The coyote disappeared before Jessica could spot him, but she couldn't stop talking about how excited she was that the animal was so close.

That evening we checked into our hotel and dined on mini market food for dinner. We talked about that first few stands and Jessica was excited to get back on the hunt the next day.

The next morning we grabbed a hearty breakfast and headed out to hunt. A short distance from town, I found a great looking spot to start off our day of calling. Two hills created a shallow canyon that emptied out to a flat area that stretched for over a mile. The wind was perfect and sitting half way up one of the hillsides would put the sun at our backs and hidden in the shadows.

We quietly hiked to the shady portion of the hill and got ready. I set Jessica up with my Ruger .204 and her shooting sticks. I was shooting my Remington 22-250 as back up. The caller was about fifty yards in front of us and anything coming in would be looking straight into the sun. I glanced over to Jessica and she gave me a thumbs-up. I nodded and told her to stay alert.

187

The Foxpro call filled the canyon with high-pitched, rodent death. We both scanned the area carefully looking for movement. After about two minutes, I spotted a fluffy white object bouncing in quickly out at 600-yards. My heart jumped. I slowly turned to Jessica and told her we had one coming in. I could see she was excited. I had her slowly move her set up a bit left to intercept the approaching coyote.

The coyote was bounding in as fast as the animal could run. Jessica finally spotted him coming quickly at about 300-yards out. I knew for her to have a chance, this animal needed to slow way down.

At around 150-yards, I dropped the volume on the call. The coyote kept coming, but slowed to a quick trot. At 120-yards, I muted the sound from the caller. The instant silence in the canyon only added to the tension. I quietly asked Jessica if she was on him. She answered, "Yes!" At 90-yards I let out a bark and the coyote slammed on the brakes. He stopped and looked up at us on the hill, right into the sun. I could see him squinting and moving his head back and forth trying to identify our position.

I was watching him through the scope of my rifle. "If you have the shot, take it," I whispered. Jessica squeezed the trigger and hit the coyote just left of center chest and he fell over dead at 90-yards.

We tried to keep calling, but Jessica was way too excited. We hiked down and picked up her prize. We were supposed to hunt our way home, but we had photos to take and a hide to take care of. That day, my youngest daughter Jessica became a hunter.

After her first successful hunt, Jessica began inserting herself into our hunting tradition. She showed more of an interest in planning future hunts and wanted to be involved in any and all outdoor activities. Her growing confidence was an absolute joy to watch.

Jessica with her first coyote taken on her very first predator hunt. I knew with her amazing marksmanship, if I could put a coyote in front of her, she would take care of the rest (Hovey 2014).

Justifying the pursuit of predators

I'm not a trophy hunter. I don't pursue animals to hang on my walls. The animals I hunt will eventually end up on our plates. Before they hunted with me, my daughters were raised on whatever meat I came home with. In fact, early on, both my daughters knew that one of the strongest reasons I hunted was to provide meat for the table.

Almost every animal I have killed as a hunter has been consumed by me and my family. Over the years, we have feasted on dove, quail, chukar, turkey, rabbit, jack rabbit, deer, pig, elk, antelope, waterfowl, crow, bobcat, pheasant, rattlesnake, bullfrogs and tree squirrel. I personally feel a responsibility to utilize the animals I hunt as food. The way I look at it is that when I consume the animals I kill the cells of those animals become a part of me and will live on in me for as long as I live. I realize this explanation takes it to a molecular level, but it is truly how I feel. The one exception to this consumption rule is when we hunt coyotes.

As a biologist, I have a working knowledge of game management and how most species, especially the predators, need to be managed to maintain healthy populations of game animals. In the wild, coyotes have few, if any natural predators. Cougars have been documented killing and consuming coyotes, but this is most certainly not their prey of choice. This means, with the exception of man, the coyote has no real natural enemies. Depending on food availability, in most wildlife areas, the coyote is the top predator of many species of animal. Add in their pack mentality and their ability to coordinate attacks, and in the absence of the wolf, coyotes are the primary killers of anything wild.

When I first began hunting coyotes in 1995, I struggled with how I could kill an animal and maybe take its pelt, but nothing more. Despite my reservations, my desire to master the art of predator calling overshadowed my internal struggle, and I continued to hunt coyotes as often as I could.

In those early years, I read a lot about coyote biology. I learned all I could about their food preferences and general habits. The original goal was to learn all I could about the animal I was chasing. An unintentional result of gathering all this research was I began to realize that hunters provide a localized amount of active management on coyotes through hunting. Most states don't have a season or limit on coyotes, and the only species management in place on coyotes is the pressure applied by sportsmen. I'm not talking about coyote control through the methods of the USDA Wildlife Services. I'm talking about one hunter's personal struggle to justify the killing of an animal without consuming it. I eventually found that it all comes down to specific species management.

The coyote has adapted very well to human presence. Patrolling at the edges of suburbia, coyotes will kill pets, threaten children and develop an aggression that always results in its eventual removal for public safety. I also discovered that there is a very real competition between coyotes and man for hunted resources. In the wild, these animals prey on the same animals I hunt to feed my family. The seasons and limits I follow as a responsible, ethical hunter, are being sabotaged by an animal that has no natural predators. In short, without managing coyotes through hunting this animal will negatively impact many groups of well-managed game animals.

My daughters are well versed in why we hunt coyotes without eating them. They understand that we are the point of the spear tasked with responsible management and that hunting is one of the strongest management tools available. They know if all hunters stopped pursuing coyotes, the game animals we hunt to feed our families would suffer. I have educated them on the biology of the coyote and they know that the best way to out-compete your competition is to control them.

Finishing what you started

When practicing marksmanship, the goal is always to hit the target. When my daughters first started shooting, they did very well in the controlled environment of target shooting. When I transitioned them to hunting, I knew there may be situations where the excitement of the hunt may affect their accuracy. A situation where I would have to show them how to dispatch an animal they had wounded during a hunt.

Even the best shots will send an off round down range and wound an animal. Ethical sportsmen will follow up the first shot, with a quick second shot to end the animal's suffering. I believe that this is all part of the responsibility of being a hunter. I've taught my daughters that if they hunt, they need to accept the responsibility of pulling the trigger. If they wounded an animal during a hunt, they needed to finish what they started.

With larger animals, finishing the job is usually just a follow up shot away. Both girls had shot coyotes early in their hunting career that required an extra shot by me to finish the animal. In both cases, the follow up shot was less than a second after their first shot. For me and my predator hunting friends, that's not unusual. We always back each other up. But in some situations, finishing the job is entirely the responsibility of the hunter who originally pulled the trigger.

Once the girls got used to the small and medium sized calibers, I moved them up to shotguns. I started them off shooting the smaller 20 gauge at ground targets. We'd shoot through a box of shells during each target session so they'd get used to the recoil and shotgun pattern at different distances.

Within one or two trips, shooting the shotgun became part of our regular shooting routine. I began bringing a box of clay pigeons out with us so they could practice on flying targets. During this early training, I was really surprised how quickly they began breaking the clay targets in midair. Once they became used to the shotgun recoil and were consistently hitting flying targets, I decided to take them out for the upcoming opener of dove season.

Since both my daughters were new to dove hunting and shooting at moving targets, I knew sooner or later they would have to dispatch a bird that wasn't completely dead once they knocked it down. I realized as the opener approached that this would be a perfect opportunity for them to confront a situation that all hunters have to deal with eventually.

During the opening morning, I watched Alyssa drop her first bird on a great crossing shot. The dove hit the ground and started flapping. At first I thought it was dead, but it soon started hopping, trying to get away. I put my shotgun away, made Alyssa's safe and we walked out to the injured bird together. I grabbed it and instantly placed my thumb and index finger around the throat and started squeezing.

I held the bird firmly with the other hand and waited for the dove to die. As I did this, I apologized to the bird out loud and told him it would be over quickly. I didn't do this because Alyssa was there. I quietly express this sentiment every time I have to finish what I started. It's that brief sad part of hunting that we all experience on occasion. I dispatched her first bird so that she could see how to do it. From then on, whenever she shot an animal and needed to finish the job, she would be responsible for that on her own. It's a hunter's responsibility.

Dealing with the different personalities of my daughters, I figured that my oldest, Alyssa would push through this requirement of a hunter and deal with the animals she chased, and I was right. I was less sure about her younger sister, Jessica.

On our next trip out, Jessica dropped a dove as it flared at the decoys. The bird hit the ground and started flapping. I could see that the dove was still alive so we walked out to it. I grabbed the bird and knelt down. Jessica knelt down next to me. I repeated the process and I told her that as hunters, we owe it to the animals to provide them with a quick and humane death. I also mentioned that it was a necessary task for any hunter and it was not something I enjoyed doing.

On the very next hunt, she dropped a bird on a great crossing shot. When the bird hit the ground, I could see that it was still alive. I instructed her to go out and get it. I didn't want to make a huge deal of it, but I did want to see how she handled it. When she reached the bird, she knelt down and held the bird firmly and dispatched it carefully. While she did, I could see her talking to the bird as I had done. As a dad, it really touched me that she made the same choice in talking to the animal as she ended its suffering.

As hunters, we strive to kill quickly. However, we also prepare ourselves for those occasions when we have to end the suffering of a wounded animal. No matter how you go about this, you absolutely need to discuss this possibility with your kids if they're going to hunt with you. I would recommend keeping it simple and not spending a great deal of time discussing it, but they definitely need to know how to finish what they started.

Jessica's first big game animal

Jessica and I eased into the steep canyon and got into position. Twenty minutes earlier I had been standing in the same spot about to hike the creek in hopes of kicking bedded pigs up towards Jessica who was positioned upstream. That all changed when I was able to sneak within yards of a group of sleeping pigs in the creek.

I carefully and quietly hiked back out, grabbed Jessica and we hiked back down into the steep canyon. The pigs were bedded about 50-yards from our position and had no idea we were there. I quietly set Jessica up on her shooting sticks and made sure she was comfortable. The pigs were piled up on top of each other under a large oak tree on the far side of the drainage. We quietly discussed her target and picked out a pig laying at the edge of the group. This was Jessica's first real big game hunt and this would be the first time she would have a large pig in her scope.

Jessica got relaxed, found her target in the scope and took the shot. A puff of dirt kicked up next to her target and every pig in the creek scattered down the drainage and out of range. I watched Jessica's pig run down the creek uninjured. Even though she clearly missed, we headed over to look for blood.

We searched the bed for a few minutes and found no sign of a hit. We returned to our perch and gathered up our gear. Jessica was silent and upset. I gave her a hug and she started to cry. She told me she really wanted that pig and she considered the shot an easy one. I calmed her down and we sat in the creek and talked about misses.

Truth be told, Jessica is an amazing shot. During her target training, as she became more proficient on the rifle, I found that I was placing targets further and further out, just to challenge her. She had no problem hitting soda cans out at 150-yards. The missed shot in the creek was a simple case of nerves.

As we talked, I told her that just three weeks previous, I had missed a far easier shot at a pig standing broadside at forty yards. I find using myself as an example when things get frustrating an excellent tool to make my daughters feel a bit easier about their failures. And make no mistake Jessica viewed the shot in the creek as a failure.

I then explained that when I take her hunting, it isn't about killing an animal. I wanted her to enjoy the outdoors, spend time with me and learn a bit about hunting. Missing shots is as much a part of hunting as the game itself. I finished our talk in the creek by letting Jessica know that misses will always happen and they are what make hitting your target so much more rewarding.

194

Right before we started the steep hike out of the creek, I told her that she needs to keep her head up and leave what just happened in the creek. I suggested she remember how she feels now and to use this experience to make her a better shot and a better hunter.

I helped her up and gave her a hug. I offered to carry her rifle and sticks, but she looked me square in the eye and told me that she carried them into the canyon, and she would carry them out. I believed that the lesson was over and we continued our lengthy hike up to the truck.

After our talk, I realized that Jessica was just like me. She's strong-willed, tough and a perfectionist. The easy miss I had experienced three weeks earlier had me sitting deep in another canyon angry and confused. I sat there for a full five minutes staring at the ground sulking. I've always been hard on myself and I started to see those same qualities in Jessica. I don't believe there's anything wrong with going though frustrating periods of wanting to better yourself in anything you do. However, the one thing I've done since childhood is to move through the anger process and take what I could from each episode to better myself. During the hike out, I decided to nurture that same behavior in Jessica. I felt that our little talk in the canyon had helped her overcome her frustration over the miss. If that wasn't enough, we were both about to see that the day's lesson wasn't over.

I was about 400-yards from the truck and Jessica was bringing up the rear. We were both red-faced and out of breath as we slowly made our way out of the steep canyon. I looked up and spotted a lone boar walking the ridge above us. He was headed towards the truck and didn't look like he had a care in the world.

Once Jessica caught up, I quietly pointed out the pig and told her if we hurry, we may get a shot. While we climbed, I kept an eye on the pig. He continued walking the ridge towards the truck and he had no idea we were there.

I reached the top of the ridge first and spotted the boar feeding up the opposite canyon. Jessica was a few minutes behind me and if the boar kept going, we may not get a shot. Jessica finally made the ridge out of breath and a bit frustrated. I told her to relax and to get her rifle on the sticks. The pig was now moving away and in ten steps he'd be over the ridge and gone.

He stopped briefly at 180-yards and gave us a quartering away shot. Jessica finally found him in the scope and said she was ready to shoot. I told her to try and tuck a bullet behind the ribs on the right side. She calmed herself, took a deep breath and fired. Through the binoculars I spotted a puff of dust come off the boar telling me she hit him. What I didn't know was how well.

We stowed our gear in the truck and headed over to where the pig was standing. I instantly found a few drops of blood on the trail. It wasn't a lot of blood, but enough to follow. Every few feet we'd find a few more drops. I then found blood on both sides of the narrow track. I showed Jessica and told her that she had hit the pig well enough that he was now bleeding out of both sides. I could tell she was excited and she stayed right at my side searching for sign. We tracked the boar for over 300-yards until the blood on the trail abruptly stopped. This is what I was afraid of. Wild pigs are tough animals with thick skin. It's not unusually for them to bleed a bit after the shot and then suddenly stop. I was hopeful at the beginning of the track, but once the blood trail disappeared my heart sank.

I was starting to circle the last spot of blood when Jessica spotted the boar directly downhill from the trail. The blood trail had abruptly stopped because the hog had died on the path and slid down the hill. Another far happier hug occurred on the side of that mountain above Jessica's first big game animal.

Just eight minutes prior to finding the downed hog, Jessica was upset and tearing up at the bottom of a canyon having experienced a missed shot at her first big game animal. Now she was smiling ear to ear. Her boar weighed about 140-pounds and her shot was perfect. The round had hit the pig just behind the last rib on the right, exiting out the left front shoulder. I told a smiling Jessica that I didn't know if I could've made the 180-yard shot.

When we talk about this hunt, we don't discuss the amazing shot Jessica made or how upset she was in the canyon. I emphasize her tenacity during that day and how despite her earlier sour mood, she did not give up. I feel kids nowadays go through frustrated periods, experience a small bit of failure and just give up on what they're doing; it's the easy way out. As parents, one of our jobs is to build character and I believe character is built through adversity. How can you know what success feels like if you don't ever experience failure? Jessica now carries that, never-give-up attitude with her no matter what activity she participates in.

Jessica, red-faced and all smiles after putting in a tough hike to take her first big game animal. Her stubbornness and tenacity were the keys to her success (Hovey 2015).

Alyssa's first big game animal

A few weeks after Jessica shot her first pig, Alyssa and I made a trip out to hunt big game in the same area. My good friend, Jose De Orta and his son Adrian joined us for the all day hunt. The plan was to search the property early for pigs moving from their feeding areas towards their beds, and then explore the ranch as the day heated up.

Over the last few months, I had been exploring the property we were hunting, trying to get a better idea of pig movement. Along with the increased hunting pressure, the late spring weather had been unseasonably hot. This meant that the pigs were traveling at night and only moving early in the morning and at last light. I knew our best chance for success would be to hunt early for moving pigs, and then kick around through their remote beds as the day heated up.

We got an early start and hunted hard during the morning. After several hard creek pushes, several miles of hiking and a handful of pig sightings, the cooler was still empty. We took a break for lunch and did a little glassing. With the day heating up, the pigs were done moving, but we weren't done hunting. With a few hours of daylight left, we decided to explore some new areas.

I drove one of the fire roads to the other side of the property. For the most part, I think we all thought the hunt was over. The road dropped off the ridge and leveled off at a heavily grazed meadow. We lazily explored the new area for about half an hour. When we reached the end of the road, we turned around and decided to head home. With the early start to the day and the long hikes, we were all worn out.

On the drive out, we spotted a small pig bed tucked away on the side of a hill. We stopped and glassed it from the road. The bed was almost perfectly round and about thirty feet in diameter. Even though the ground surrounding the bed was turned over and it looked fresh, I wasn't convinced that a pig would be bedded up so close to the road. Jose thought differently.

Over the last few hunts on the property, I've noticed that most of the hunters were done hunting and off the ranch by late morning. While most were convinced that the pigs were done moving by this time, I'd spend the midday searching for occupied pig beds. Tucked away in deep canyons and usually off the beaten path, pigs would move into these areas to escape the heat and the hunting pressure. Playing the wind and searching for fresh sign, I'd sneak into these bedding areas and stalk within feet of sleeping pigs. I called it kicking through beds, and early in the season it had been a very successful technique for locating pigs any time of day.

I drove across the meadow and parked about 250-yards from the bed. Jose volunteered to hike to the spot and kick through it. I got the kids set up with their rifles and shooting sticks, facing downhill and perpendicular to the bed. We watched Jose and we waited.

Jose made his way to the top of the bed and started tossing sticks and rocks into the thick vegetation. The kids were ready and excited, but I still believed Jose was wasting his time. I just felt that the bed was too small and too close to the main road to hold any animals.

Through the binoculars I watched as he moved through the bed, kicking the thick brush and throwing things. He was just about in the center of the bush when he stopped suddenly. Jose was chest deep and looking in front of him. All of a sudden a large boar broke cover near the edge of the small bed and headed out downhill as fast as a pig could run.

Alyssa and Adrian spotted the pig and started lining up on him. The pig was running straight away from Jose and within 50-yards it would be racing broadside right across their firing line about 150-yards out. Within seconds the kids would have an open opportunity to kill their first pig.

For a few seconds, we all just watched, waiting for the pig to run into position. Then, without any provocation, the boar suddenly changed course and started running directly at us. The pig was about 150-yards out and closing fast. I told the kids to get the boar in their scopes and to start firing. Alyssa fired first and hit the pig in the head. A puff of dust exploded off the animal's skull, but he never slowed down. Adrian fired next and hit the running boar in the front left leg. The boar stumbled slightly, but regained its pace and kept coming.

The next two shots by the kids were clean misses. Despite the firing, the pig kept running right at us. As the pig closed the distance, he veered off to our left at about 20-yards and kept running. To keep things safe and since the pig had changed direction, the kids disengaged. My rifle, an older Marlin 30-30, was sitting in the rear of the truck with a spent shell stuck in the action and essentially useless. I grabbed Alyssa's 30-06 and fired a quick shot as the boar crested a hill, hitting him in the back leg.

Since the pig was now clear of where we were and headed towards cover, Jose started firing. With one amazing shot, he hit the boar on the run with a shot to the vitals. I added one more, as the pig disappeared over a small rise.

The kids and I jumped into the truck and raced over to where we had last seen the pig. When it disappeared, it was headed out into a grazed field at the base of some rolling hills. If he escaped into foothills, we'd never find him.

Driving faster than I should, we rounded the hill and easily spotted the running pig against a field of dry grass. He was still moving fast and headed towards the heavy brush of the low hills and his escape. I made a wide loop and cut the pig off. He changed direction, cut behind the vehicle and made a quick push to make it to the hills. I hit him again with our last rifle bullet at 70-yards. He stumbled, but kept trotting. I handed Alyssa the rifle and ran towards the escaping pig, my .357 revolver firmly gripped. The wounded boar tried to navigate a steep hill and tipped over, sliding back to level ground. He made a weak attempt to get up, but a finishing shot to the back of the neck with my pistol at ten feet concluded the shooting.

I stood over the warrior pig and looked at the wounds. Alyssa's head shot hit the pig in the center of the forehead and glanced off the thick skull. Adrian had broken the front left leg but that did little to slow the pig down. Jose's long shot hit the pig dead center and barely missed the lungs. My two quick fleeing shots glanced off the right ham and were only flesh wounds. My last rifle shot hit both lungs and broke the off shoulder. The close shot behind the head ended it all. From the first shot to the last, the entire episode lasted less than a minute.

The kids were back at the truck and I was alone with the battle-scarred boar. I knelt next to the animal and patted the chest. I'm not ashamed to say that I openly apologized to that dead animal for the excess shots, and I thanked him for the meat that would eventually go to feed two families. As I reviewed the scenario in my head, I felt that, under the circumstances, we had done all we could to end the event quickly.

Since the kids had hit the pig first, it was their first confirmed big game kill. With the rushing pig and the chaos, the kids handled themselves safely the entire time. They disengaged when the pig had changed direction and only took shots when I instructed them to. Beyond killing their first big game animal, Jose and I were far prouder of how the young hunters had handled themselves in the wild situation.

We took some photos and then showed Alyssa and Adrian how to field dress their first pig. Despite the wounds, we were able to harvest all four hams and two back straps. To complete the experience, Alyssa and Adrian wanted to hike the meat of their first pig back to the truck. The first of many I'm sure.

Boar at war! Adrian De Orta and Alyssa with a huge boar they brought down together. Beyond the taking of the pig, the way they safely handled themselves during the wild hunt was impressive to watch (Hovey 2015).

Jessica and the badger

We all have those animals that we consider our nemesis; animals that have been tough to kill, hard to hunt or for one reason or another, just plain difficult to acquire. Mine has always been the common badger. I've been intrigued with the stocky creature ever since I first encountered one during an overnight solo hunt years ago. When I was eighteen and branching out on my own, I would frequently hunt this piece of public land north of where we lived. Armed with my trusty Ruger 10/22, I would hike the hills looking for rabbits and ground squirrels.

One afternoon I was sitting on a grazed hill looking over the squirrel mounds across the canyon, when I spotted a larger animal completely focused on aggressively digging a hole below me. Through the scope, I was convinced it was a raccoon and I hiked down the hill to check it out.

The animal was almost completely underground, with only its rear and tail sticking out of the hole. He was so focused on digging that I was able to walk right up to him undetected. As a goof, I poked him with the butt of my rifle. Without warning, he instantly extracted himself from the hole and came at me with far more aggression than I ever expected. The retaliation was so sudden, that I had no time to turn around to escape and had to back pedal to keep from getting mauled. The badger growled loudly as it chased me down the canyon. All I remember was seeing three-inch claws, gnashing teeth and a black and white head coming at me as fast as he could run. After over 100-yards, the badger finally peeled off and escaped into another hole. I remember sitting down exhausted and a bit scared. I have no idea why using my rifle never even entered my mind, and I know it's impossible, but when I remember this episode, I'm almost certain the badger chased me running only on its back legs.

Ever since what I call 'the badger' incident, I have been almost obsessed with killing one. Here in California, we do have a season for them, but I've seen more dead badgers on the road than I have live ones, and the live ones I've seen have always been outside the hunting season for them.

My good friend, Ed Davis has known about my badger quest for quite some time and frequently makes fun of me for it. A few years back, during a predator hunt in Nevada, Ed got to see firsthand just how bad my badger fever was. At that time, non-resident hunters didn't need a license to hunt predators or non-game mammals in the silver state, and Ed had mentioned that we could possibly run into a badger during our trip.

One afternoon, we were hiking to a small bluff to call coyotes, when the dirt below a bush in front of me came to life. With coyotes on the brain, I figured we had kicked up a bedded coyote. As the dirty creature retreated, dirt and dust slipped from its hide revealing the striped face of a large badger. I knelt down and found the running animal in the scope at 40-yards, fired and missed. Surging with adrenaline, I short-stroked the next round, causing a jam. For some reason my good friend Ed decided that I had my chance and started firing. I finally cleared the jam and found the badger perched at his hole looking back at me. That snapshot in time still haunts me. I steadied my aim and put the .204 round right over his back at 60-yards. The badger escaped unharmed down his hole. Ed's uncontrollable laughter punctuated the entire event. After that, with the infrequent sightings and my missed opportunities, I figured getting a badger just wasn't in the cards for me.

Towards the end of 2015, Jessica and I were on a solo hunting trip. It was getting close to the end of the season for us, and I was just glad to be out with my daughter. After driving around, searching for jack rabbits, we decided to hike to a rocky area to glass for game. On the last trip, Jessica had shot really well and harvested her first limit of cottontails. With a new rabbit recipe in mind, she was anxious to add a few more to the cooler.

I was doing the glassing and Jessica had the .17 HMR she won in the forum contest on the sticks. With not much moving, we were just sitting there enjoying another day outside. I can remember looking over at her as she peered through the scope at the distant hill. At the age of thirteen, she had come a long way since we had started. The timid little girl that was afraid to try anything new had been pushed aside to allow the tough and stubborn Jessica through. I smiled thinking how much like me she was. I can also remember having this overwhelming thankfulness that we had both stayed persistent during this journey. How I always made sure to ask her if she wanted to go, even after countless refusals. How she had decided on her own when she was ready. Now, those minor hurdles lay like clothes that no longer fit on the path behind her totally forgotten.

I was lost in the memories, when Jessica spotted something. "Hey Daddy, what is that?" I raised the binoculars and found what she was looking at. My blood went cold. There, 150-yards away, posing in the same exact position as the last one I had taken a shot at years ago was a large badger.

In seconds, the heartwarming reminiscing was shattered. As we watched, the badger took off over the next ridge. We grabbed our gear, made the .17 safe and started running towards the rocky canyon.

We reached the spot where the badger had been standing less than a minute after we spotted him. At first we didn't see him, and then Jessica spotted him cresting the next ridge over about 300-yards away. I couldn't believe he had covered that much ground in the time it had taken us to get to the ridge. As I watched him disappear over the next hill, I silently cursed my luck with the wily badger.

Jessica and I hiked back to the truck and drove out the way we had come in. We both kept our eyes open as we moved through the canyon. We came to the end of the two-track and I decided to head to another area to once again look for rabbits. As we drove I glance over to the ridge where we had last seen the badger and there he was, perched at the edge of his hole watching us 150-yards out.

I pulled over and grabbed the only rifle I brought for the day, my Ruger 17 HMR. I steadied the rifle on the sticks and found the badger in the scope. He had turned around and was looking over his shoulder at me, quartering away. I could feel my heart pounding as I steadied the crosshairs, aiming for the off shoulder. I slowly squeezed the trigger and heard the bullet hit the badger. He stumbled, got back up and disappeared into his hole. My heart sank. I knew if he made it to his hole, I probably wouldn't find him.

We drove over and found the large dirt hole in the middle of an open field. A streak of blood was next to it, but no badger. I then looked into the three foot deep hole and saw the back half of the animal. One poke confirmed he was done and I pulled my first badger out of the hole.

We took a few photos and then decided to head home. Beyond killing my first badger, it was a great day out hunting with Jessica. We spent most of our time driving around, talking and enjoying the day. I also explained to her that since she had spotted the badger, it wasn't so much my first badger, but ours. She seemed to like that.

I have been chasing a badger for a very long time. With all the close encounters and misses, I was thankful that I was finally able to add a large badger skull to my collection. It was extra special that Jessica, my tough and confident daughter was at my side during that hunt. Having her there with me was far more important than killing the badger.

Jessica was definitely my lucky charm during our badger hunt. Spending time with her outside was the highlight of the day; the badger was just a bonus (Hovey 2015).

Wyoming deer

While my daughters were chasing wild pigs in the foothills of California, our 2015 group application to hunt antelope in Wyoming was rolling around the random drawing drum. The year before, I was lucky enough to draw a Wyoming antelope tag for the fall 2014 season. A few days before the opener, I drove to Cody and met up with my good friend, Darrin Bergen. After some brief scouting and a lengthy stalk, I was able to kill a nice buck on opening day. While I was quartering out the animal, Darrin suggested that I put my daughters in for a group draw for antelope the following year. Since my first antelope application attempt had been successful, I was hopeful that my next trip out to Wyoming would be with my daughters.

We were on vacation, soaking up some sun on the beach when I received the draw results on my phone. I followed the link and saw that our group application was not successful in the antelope draw. I was heartbroken. Darrin had mentioned that it was pretty lucky for me to get drawn the first time I put in the year before and that I shouldn't get my hopes up. Most of my hunting buddies know I'm a pretty lucky hunter, and even though the odds were low for getting a group draw for antelope, I was very hopeful. Unfortunately, sitting at the beach on vacation with my little secret, I wasn't feeling very lucky.

I called the girls over and told them the news. I explained that without the tags, we weren't going to Wyoming. Jessica had tears in her eyes.

When I contacted Darrin and told him we had blanked on antelope, he mentioned that maybe we could pick up some leftover deer tags. He told me he'd look into it and let me know. At that point, I figured a trip to Wyoming in 2015 wasn't going to happen.

A few months later Darrin gave me a call and said that there were four leftover tags available for the zone near his hometown of Cody. I jumped on line and secured three, either sex deer tags for Zone X and I let the girls find them in the mail. With a renewed sense of excitement, me and my daughters loaded up the truck and headed to Wyoming in the beginning of November to hunt deer.

On the morning of the third day we found ourselves perched on the edge of a bluff looking into the canyon below. The mood was somber. We had hunted hard the previous two days on public BLM land, and while deer had been spotted, we had seen more hunters than animals. The weather had been brutal, with high winds and very cold temperatures that tested our dedication and resolve. Despite these tough conditions, my daughters stayed positive and kept on hunting.

Now, sitting on the same very popular plot of public land, we had to deal with a missed opportunity to end the trip. During the walk in, I had spotted a single doe making her way up a private ravine, getting ready to enter the public land plot. Our tags were good for either sex deer and this late in the game I figured it was time to put some meat in the freezer.

I grabbed Jessica and had her get ready if the doe came over to public land. While we waited, Alyssa got our attention and carefully pointed off to our right. A dozen deer were perched on the same ravine watching us. I slowly lifted my binoculars and noticed that three of the deer were bucks and two of them were far bigger than any we had ever seen hunting in California.

The herd watched us for about 30-seconds and then slowly disappeared down the ravine. We grabbed our gear and quickly raced to the edge of the canyon to cut them off. By the time we got set up, the last buck was crossing the creek bottom 210-yards below us. Jessica quickly got her rifle on her sticks and said she had the moving buck in her scope. I whistled loudly and the deer stopped perfectly broadside. I told Jessica to take the shot if she had it. Less than a second later she squeezed the trigger and missed the buck less than an inch high. My heart dropped into my stomach. The deer raced across the shallow canyon and was gone within seconds.

Both my daughters are passionate about hunting and the outdoors, and they don't take missed shots well. Jessica leaned her forehead down, resting it on the rifle scope and started to cry. I rubbed her back and told her it was a long shot. I also told her she was less than an inch from killing that deer. This didn't seem to make her feel any better. To add insult to injury, about 45-seconds after her shot, we heard another shot ring out from the valley the buck had escaped to.

Earlier that morning, I had offered to let the girls sleep in since we had hunted so hard the previous two days. They both declined the offer and convinced me to get up early and keep trying. Now with the missed shot, cold weather and only six hours left to hunt, we all believed we were headed back to California with empty coolers and unfilled tags.

The three of us sat at the edge of the ravine for another thirty minutes. Jessica eventually overcame the miss and started feeling better. I explained to her that misses will always happen and that she needed to deal with them in a mature and productive way. She agreed and slowly started to put it behind her. I gave her a hug, and even though I felt like her shot was the last opportunity we'd have at taking a deer, I told her the hunt wasn't over and she should never give up. She smiled through the tears and nodded.

With some encouragement, Jessica calmed herself and pushed the miss to the back of her mind where she'd remember it forever. Since the morning deer movement was over, we were about to head back to the truck when we noticed a hunter over in the next valley struggling to get a deer back to his vehicle by himself. Through the binoculars, I could see the older gentleman pulling the deer by its small rack up an incline. The buck he was wrestling with was the one Jessica had missed earlier. We decided to drive over and give him a hand.

By the time we got over to the hunter, he had managed to handle most of the heavy lifting by himself but he appreciated the offer to help him out. We talked to him for a bit and he mentioned that the ridge he was on had been very lucky for him over the years. He strongly suggested that we return to the same area for an evening hunt. Both my daughters seemed excited at this new plan and with a renewed sense of hope, the three us got back into the truck and headed for Grannies' in the nearby town of Cody for pancakes. Little did we realize that we had already set in motion a set of circumstances that would change our plans for the rest of the day.

The road into the hunting area is a well worn two-track and as we made our way back to the main road, I noticed a truck coming our way. I pulled over to let him pass and noticed that it was a Wyoming Game and Fish warden. He stopped, checked our tags and talked to us for a bit. He introduced himself as Bill and he thought it was great that I had driven all the way from California to hunt with my daughters. He asked us what our plans were and I told him we were going to hunt one more evening and then head home early the next day. He pulled out a business card and started writing on the back of it. He handed it to me and told me to give Alan, a land manager for a large piece of private land a call. He seemed confident that Alan would allow us access to the property to finish off our hunting trip. Bill mentioned we may at least have an opportunity to fill one of our Wyoming deer tags before we headed home.

I shook Bill's hand and thanked him. He got back into his truck and continued on down the road. I looked at the card, and while I was optimistic about the contact, I knew we didn't have a lot of time left to hunt.

Alan picked up the phone on the second ring and gladly agreed to let Alyssa, Jessica and I hunt the property he managed. Over the phone he gave us directions to his shop where we could pick up the land owner's hunting permit, get a map and take a tour of the property. Since Alan was busy, he arranged for his maintenance man, Chuni to give us a tour. Alan told us to be careful, wished us luck and hung up the phone.

Within an hour of meeting Bill, the game warden up on the very public BLM land, we were in Chuni's work truck getting a detailed view of a very large piece of private property. At the end of the loop, Chuni had us fill out the forms and gave us our map. Since we were already on the property and the weather looked perfect, the girls and I decided to start hunting immediately. While we each held non-resident deer tags, my goal was to see if I could get my daughters on their very first deer.

We slowly drove down the perimeter road looking for deer. The property was a mix of agricultural fields, and native habitat, and we were lucky enough to have access to it all.

I crossed over a wooden bridge and started traveling the perimeter of a cornfield. We hadn't gone 50-feet when Alyssa spotted a bedded deer in the old corn. She quietly got out and moved to the edge of the field. She got set up on her shooting sticks and got comfortable. I could see the bedded deer's ear, but Alyssa needed the deer to stand to take the shot. When she was ready, I made a bleating noise and the deer stood up looking our way. Alyssa steadied herself and hit the deer perfectly at 90-yards.

The deer took off, spitting blood from both sides of its body. It then disappeared in the heavy brush of the cornfield. I was very confident in her shot, but the dense corn had me hoping we didn't lose the animal.

We quickly found blood and tracked it back to where Alyssa had taken the shot. The first blood spatter was frothy and bright red; lung. We slowly followed the excessive blood trail for about fifty feet and found Alyssa's first deer piled up in a corn row.

All three of us were ecstatic. After a long trip, we finally had a deer on the ground. We took some pictures and quartered out the deer. Alyssa filled out her first ever deer tag and attached it to one of the legs. We loaded the meat into the cooler and headed out again. It was 1:30 PM.

I stayed on the same road and we slowly drove the edge of the field. Jessica was up next. Since we had spotted one animal bedded in the cornfield, we figured that many of the deer may be staying on the property and bedding down in the agricultural fields. Chuni had mentioned that deer would frequently bed down in the center of the agriculture fields and may be difficult to spot. He was right. Alyssa had spotted the tip of one ear while we were driving and I think we all realized animals were going to be tough to see in the thick farm fields.

I moved beyond a grove of trees near the next cornfield. Jessica was searching when she suddenly stiffened up. She asked me to back up a bit. She Looked through the binoculars and spotted a bedded doe out in the center of the field over 300-yards away. Her young eyes had gotten a glimpse of an object about the size of a soda can as we were driving. Now, examining the deer through the binoculars, I could see it was a large doe and she was looking right at us. She was only visible when we were positioned looking straight down the three-foot wide row.

I backed the truck up so that we were out of view and we waited a few minutes. There was a swath of native habitat between us and the edge of the cornfield. I felt pretty confident, that with the wind, Jessica and I could drop down off the ridge, stalk to within range and give her a shot.

We left Alyssa on the ridge to spot for us. Jessica and I headed down into a thick creek bottom and quietly made our way to the field edge. After ten minutes of quiet stalking, we got to within 200-yards of the bedded deer. With her position in the center of the field, we really couldn't get any closer undetected.

I set up Jessica's shooting sticks and she found the deer in her scope. With the heavy brush at the edge of the field, she would have to stand for the shot; something she was not used to. The doe was looking our way and despite being bedded, she presented enough of a target to take a shot. Jessica steadied herself and slowly squeezed the trigger.

The doe popped to her feet and it looked to me that Jessica had missed low. The deer ran about thirty feet through the thick cornfield and stopped broadside in an open area. The silhouette of the deer was visible, but she had several stalks obscuring a clear view. Jessica loaded another round and found the standing deer in her scope. I told her to shoot right through the corn at the deer's vitals. At the shot, I heard the bullet hit the deer and then I lost sight of it.

Jessica was convinced that she had missed both shots. I told her that the second shot hit the deer and we needed to head out there and look for blood. To avoid losing track of where the doe was I took two landmarks before we headed out. I had Alyssa stay where she was so she could guide us in from her elevated perch near the truck.

Jessica and I made our way out to where we had last seen the deer. I walked around the area and didn't see any blood. After a few minutes with no sign, I glance back to where Alyssa was. I could see her looking at us through the binoculars, and she looked like she was waving. I looked through my binoculars and I could see that she was pointing us further right. I took three steps and saw a square patch of blood. I called Jessica over and told her to walk towards it. A few steps later we found her deer.

Jessica's doe was massive. We tracked the blood back to her bed and realized Jessica had hit her with the first shot with a lethal hit right through the neck. We cleaned her up and took some pictures. I signaled Alyssa to bring the meat packs out and we started quartering up the deer. The three of celebrated our success deep in the abandon corn field in the middle of nowhere. I told both of the girls that I was proud of how they hadn't given up, and how despite the tough conditions, they kept hunting. The take home message of the day was that hard work and dedication was rewarded.

We loaded up Jessica's deer and kept searching the property. I was satisfied with my daughter's filling their tags, but the girls made it clear that we still had one more deer to find. With less than an hour of daylight left, we kept slow driving near the agriculture fields searching for deer.

I had just decided that we were done, and was making my way to the edge of the property when I spotted a pair of ears in the thick vegetation near the creek edge. Through the binoculars I could see a doe looking right at us about 120-yards out. With less than thirty minutes of daylight left, I decided this was probably going to be my last chance. Through the scope, all I could see was the deer's face. I felt solid on the sticks, so I pit the crosshairs on the nose and squeezed the trigger. The deer fell from sight and was done. As the sun set over our last evening in Wyoming, I added the quarters of deer number three to the cooler in the back of the truck.

Earlier that morning we were on a ridge after a tough miss, a bit disappointed and definitely at the end of our hunt. My daughters hunted in tough conditions and never quit. Together, on the edge of that canyon, a bit defeated, we decided to go help a fellow hunter out. That delay in our departure brought us into contact with Warden Bill and eventually to our unbelievable hunt. My daughters persevered and stayed positive. As their father, I was beyond proud of them and it was great to see their tenacity rewarded. Our last hunting day in Wyoming will be a day none of us will ever forget.

Alyssa is all smiles with her Wyoming deer. My daughters hunted hard on public land for three days and never gave up. A chance meeting with a warden was the key to western hospitality and hunting success (Hovey 2015).

After a tough miss earlier in the day, Jessica once again relied on her tenacity and never quit. Her reward was shooting the largest deer of the trip (Hovey 2015).

Our first double

During the first week of 2016, Alyssa and I headed out to the desert to do some predator calling. With 2015 being such a successful hunting year for me and my daughters, we were looking forward to hopefully put an exclamation point on our season of firsts.

During the previous year, both Alyssa and Jessica had taken their first big game animals, and had a successful out of state deer hunt. With the 2015-2016 hunting season coming to a close, me and my daughters already had hunting trips planned for the coming year. We're headed to northern California for their first spring turkey hunt in late March. We'll once again concentrate on wild pigs at the ranch in late spring, and a return trip to Wyoming to hunt with my good friend Darrin is planned for the fall.

As we drove through the desert, Alyssa and I talked about past trips and all the adventures we've had in the outdoors. I thought about how both Alyssa and Jessica had basically grown up in the arid Mojave. From shooting, to hunting, to night runs for snakes, my daughters have learned the basics of being tough, outdoorswomen in the desert that I so dearly love.

We pulled off near one of our favorite calling spots and looked around. The conditions were perfect and I picked out an elevated spot for our first stand. In the early morning sun, the vast dry drainage just screamed coyote. We hiked in quietly and set up. I hiked downhill about 40-yards and set out the call. Back at the stand, Alyssa would be covering the left side of the dry creek bed and I'd cover the right. The rising sun was behind us and the wind was in our face. Our elevated perch gave us an amazing view of a half a mile of perfect predator habitat. I looked over at Alyssa and smiled. She just nodded, pure excitement in her eyes. She understood that our calling spot was perfect.

The caller had been screaming non-stop for about ten minutes. I had been picking apart the terrain, looking for a cat's face, when Alyssa whispered 'coyote!' I looked left and saw a large, light colored coyote racing in towards the call. I usually like to mute the call when predators are running in to make them pause for the shot. This animal wasn't going to stop for anything. When he got to the call, he caught my scent and reversed course, leaving as fast as he had come in. That's when I spotted the second coyote.

A smaller, darker coyote was stopped out at bout 90-yards just watching. The larger coyote raced right by the second and kept going. I swung over on the second one, as Alyssa adjusted to the running coyote. I let out a lone howl, and the running animal started loping to a stop. Seconds later he stopped broadside and looked back at the hill. I put the crosshairs on the second animal and fired. Alyssa shot at the exact same time, and was convinced that we had hit the same animal. I told her that we had two coyotes come in and both were down. She was so focused on the first one, that she never saw the second one standing in the low brush just watching.

After the animals were down, I realized that this was the first true double for me and Alyssa. We collected our coyotes and admired the animals. Alyssa's was a beast and she wanted the pelt and the skull. After a few photos, we loaded up and headed to the next stand.

Alyssa couldn't stop talking about our first double. With the quick action, I was beyond impressed with her composure. She easily moved on the animal while it was running, waited for it to present a good shot and dropped it less than a second after it stopped. There was no doubting that after eight years in the field, Alyssa has turned into an amazing hunter.

We quietly hiked into our next stand and got set up on the side of a hill. We weren't as hidden on this stand, but we had a great view of the desert floor. With Alyssa on the left and me covering the right, I started calling.

Ten minutes in I spotted a coyote hard charging into the call. He was coming in on my side as fast as a coyote could run. Without moving, I whispered to Alyssa that we had one coming in. She spotted him and instantly swung her set up towards the right. With the sun lighting us up, the coyote had no problem spotting her movement and he slammed on the brakes at about 150-yards. He turned himself inside out leaving and disappeared back into the desert shrub.

I looked over at Alyssa and smiled. She knew she had moved too soon and tipped off the approaching animal. "I moved too soon, huh?" She sighed deeply, a bit frustrated. I didn't need to answer her.

Ironically, a few stands later, I punctured a tire in the back hills. Alyssa took care of the spare and changed it out completely on her own. We headed back to town and grabbed some food. Even though the day had ended early, we talked about the two first stands all the way home. On the highway, I thanked Alyssa for coming out with me. Like she always did, she thanked me for taking her. I thought about our journey that started in 2007. I thought about how nervous I was during our very first trip out, and how Alyssa eventually convinced me to relax. I thought about all I've taught Alyssa and Jessica over the years, including how to change a flat. I also thought about all I've learned from them.

I looked back over at Alyssa and felt a flood of emotion. My daughters are my life and having them at my side as we travel the country hunting makes me so thankful. I understand that I made the decision to bring my daughters out with me, but their willingness to let me lead them down the hunter's path, is a gift that is beyond value. I reached over and put my hand on her shoulder to get her attention. She looked over and for a brief second, I saw the little girl that had started this journey with me. I felt tears well up in my eyes as I smiled at her. "No baby, thank you!"

Me and Alyssa with our first predator double. After years of practice and training, I've watched my daughters mature into responsible, capable hunters (Hovey 2016).

Jessica with her very first cottontail rabbit limit taken during a spring hunt. Her strong, independent personality developed during this journey and it was amazing to watch (Hovey 2015).

Me and the girls getting ready to chase wild pigs (Hovey 2015).

This was Alyssa's last trip out with me as an observer. The following week she took her hunter's safety test and we picked up her junior hunting license (Hovey 2011).

The girls and I on an adventure bear hunt in Idaho. We took ATV's back to the hunting area and hiked through heavy snow. Not a shot was taken, but this photo was well worth the effort (Hovey 2012).

The end of a great crow hunt with Alyssa. It didn't matter what game we were chasing, Alyssa was up for any type of hunt (Hovey 2015).

Jessica hauling pork out of the canyon. She taught me so much during this process (Hovey 2015).

My daughters sitting over a pig bed. I'm proud of the young ambassadors they've become (Hovey 2015).

Jessica and Alyssa hunting rabbits with my good friend, Darrin Bergen in Wyoming. My daughters really enjoyed hunting out of state with Uncle Darrin (Hovey 2015).

Jessica loved looking for snakes before she became interested in hunting. This monster rattlesnake was taken on a quick trip near our home (Hovey 2011).

A desert pin cushion. My daughters and I getting ready to call a predator stand (Hovey 2013).

Another crow hunt with Alyssa. If game was within her range, it didn't stand a chance (Hovey 2014).

My daughters dragging Alyssa's first deer back to the truck. It didn't matter what needed to be done during this process, they got in there and got dirty (Hovey 2015).

Making memories in the deep canyons of California. It has always been about the adventure and far less about what is loaded into the cooler (Hovey 2015).

The results of letting Alyssa run through a pig bed. She kicked it up and I killed it on the run. A great day in the field (Hovey 2015).

Jessica using her .17 HMR rifle she won as Hunter of the Year to harvest a cottontail rabbit (Hovey 2015).

Alyssa using her Hunter of the Year .17 HMR rifle to harvest her first cottontail limit (Hovey2015).

Jessica and Alyssa enjoying a successful crow hunt with Adrian De Orta (Hovey 2014).

The girls putting their offseason practice to practical use (Hovey 2015).

Jessica with her monster Wyoming doe. She braved the harsh weather and never quit (Hovey 2015).

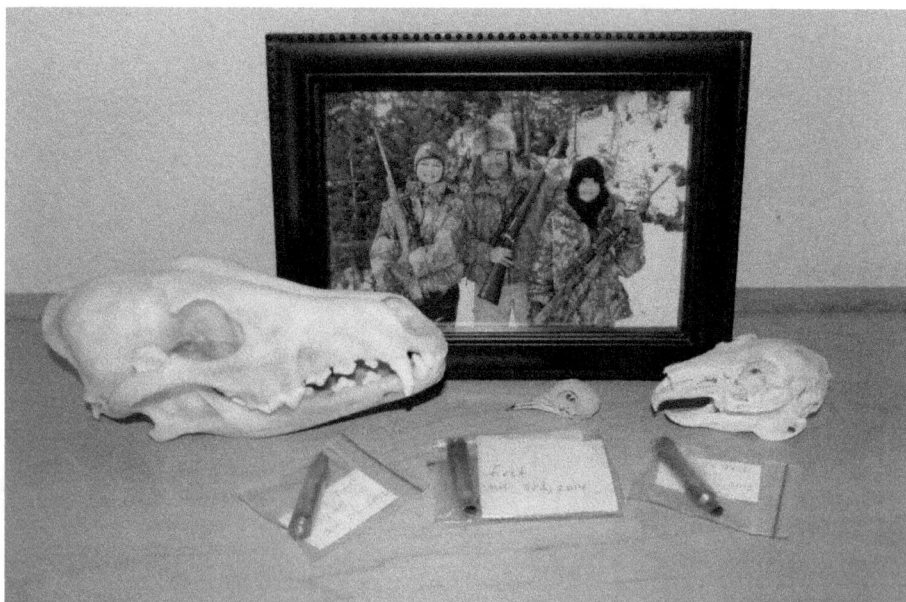

Trophies of their hunts. Whether it was photos, skulls or brass, I always encouraged their collections (Hovey 2015).

Alyssa with her first turkey taken on a spring hunt in northern California (Hovey 2016).

Jessica on point, getting ready to call predators (Hovey 2014).

Jessica at my side on her first big game hunt when I shot this boar. This is one of my favorite photos of us in the field (Hovey 2015).

Whether it was scouting, hiking or field dressing, Alyssa and Jessica assisted in all parts of the process. They know that hard work and dedication will yield rewards (Hovey 2015).

A PARTING THOUGHT

Without a doubt, this has been an amazing journey, and one I will treasure for the rest of my life. Not because my daughters are now hunters, but because of all the memories we've built in the outdoors. When I first began teaching Alyssa and Jessica, I never imagined they'd stay interested all the way to the hunting level. Over the years, I've watch them become self confident individuals, conscientious stewards of the resource and responsible hunters. The little girls that used to sit next to me on calling stands and watch, and fall asleep on the ride home are now my hunting partners. I fully believe that their early development was supported and enhanced by the self confidence and self esteem they collected during their training. My only regret is that my dad didn't get a chance to see what strong young women his granddaughters have become.

Through this stage of life, I've raised Alyssa and Jessica just like I was raised. I followed my father's footsteps through much of this process and am forever grateful that in memory, he was there to guide me. He passed away unexpectedly in 2007, the same year we started, but not before he met my young daughters, who came to know him as Papa. With a firm understanding of what this man meant to me, I vowed to show my girls much of what he showed me. He didn't tell me how to live; he lived and let me watch him do it.

My daughters now write reports on the benefits of hunting and the importance of resource management. They take wild game to school for their lunches and wear their camo with pride. With a solid foundation of wildlife behavior, firearm safety and good hunter ethics, they are both capable young women that also happened to be hunters. What they've become sets them apart from the normal high school crowd, and I can see that they seriously enjoy this individuality. When I discuss this period of time with anyone, I don't tell them that I've trained two hunters; I explain that I have created two hunting ambassadors that will educate those that wish to know more.

I believe that it's every sportsman's obligation to spread our positive role at every opportunity. It is our job to change the negative view some may have of the outdoorsmen. We are all ambassadors and we must sway the undecided and ignore those that refuse our message. The best way to approach this is to get involved and educate with patience and kindness.

The conservation-oriented movement has seen the creation of many conservation groups by dedicated sportsmen that specifically benefit game animals all over the country. These organizations, through sound science, extensive volunteer programs and education, have given those interested in preserving our hunting heritage, access to conservation. These countless groups have also given value to North American game animals, and value is how our world conserves a resource. I urge all sportsmen to discover their interests and to join these organizations. Whether you donate time or money, getting involved in conservation at any level should be a high priority for any sportsman. Involvement is our voice, and in a time where the future of our hunting heritage is being threatened, everyone needs to speak.

Support is also needed at a sportsmen's level. Hunting is a brother and sisterhood, and I can't emphasize enough how sportsmen and women from all over the country need to embrace any type of legal hunting they encounter. Lead by example and teach your children if it's legal and ethical, we should stand united. We need to build and establish a solid pillar of support for all our hunting brothers and sisters who follow the rules, whether you've participated in that type of hunting or not. If it's a legal form of pursuit, we should all stand in support of each other and tolerate and embrace the differences.

As parents, we must be aware that our kids are always watching what we do and how we act. In the field, they will look to follow your example, good or bad. The simple act of demonstrating good ethics in front of them will go a long way in teaching them the proper behavior of a sportsman. When they're old enough to understand, explain to them how hunter ethics fit into the role of a conservationist. Use simple hunting situations to illustrate choices, both good and bad, to emphasize your point of view. A strong and solid foundation of ethics will inspire new hunters to strive for conservation, support resource management, and not measure their hunting success by what they kill, but rather, by the experience.

As sportsmen, we all have the knowledge and understanding of how important and enjoyable our outdoor heritage is to us and our families. We cannot simply participate in these activities without educating those around us that don't. I feel that it's our responsibility to teach the next generation what we know. It's the only way to increase involvement and popularity in the hunting and fishing activities. If we don't get our children involved, these activities will go away. We need to show our kids the world beyond the sidewalk so they can see and more importantly feel how important our outdoor heritage is. It is time for us all to take our youth back outside.

ABOUT THE AUTHOR

Born and raised in California, Tim's interest in the outdoors started early. Building off that interest, he entered college and earned a Bachelor's of Science degree in environmental biology. Feeling like he needed more specific experience, Tim continued on and earned a Master's of Science degree in marine biology.

After college, Tim worked as a marine biologist for a consulting firm and a marine hatchery facility. In 1999, he was hired as a marine biologist by the California Department of Fish and Game. Since then, Tim has worked for several department programs before finally becoming the Department's species expert for the threatened and endangered fish, amphibians and reptiles of southern California.

Writing has always been a very important part of Tim's personal and professional life. As a biologist, scientific research papers are a part of most projects, and he has authored or co-authored dozens of peer-reviewed articles as an environmental scientist.

Personal writing projects resulted in Tim's first book, Out in the Field, discovering a career in field biology, published in 2012. Describing his early field experiences and adventures in Baja California, the text is a descriptive view of what it takes to work in the field sciences.

While Tim enjoys the larger book projects, his real passion is writing about hunting and fishing adventures for several national magazines. Beginning in 2000, Tim has written topics covering all forms of hunting and fishing for Outdoor California, Saltwater Sportsman, Predator Xtreme, Predator Nation, American Shooting Journal, Western Outdoor News, California Sportsman, California's Hunter Education Quarterly and The Firing Line. The glossy pages of the magazines are where he first started describing his outdoor adventures with his daughters.

Along with these writing projects, in 2002 Tim launched Dermestid Inc. a unique and successful internet business that supplies flesh-eating, dermestid beetles all over the globe.

Museums, hobbyist and taxidermists use these specialized beetles to clean skulls and bones for display.

Tim currently lives in southern California with his beautiful and supportive wife, Cheryl, and his two outdoor daughters, Alyssa and Jessica.

OUT IN THE FIELD
Discovering a career in field biology

Tim E. Hovey

Out in the field chronicles the many adventures of an outdoor career that a large percentage of the general public may never see. Tim scrapes away the romantic and often misunderstood view of marine scientists, and takes an honest and often humorous look at what it actually takes to become a field biologist. while Tim was completely aware that this training would eventually lead him to a job working outdoors, he had no idea that on several occasions it would also risk his life.

Available at:

www.dermestidinc.com/Out_in_the_Field.html

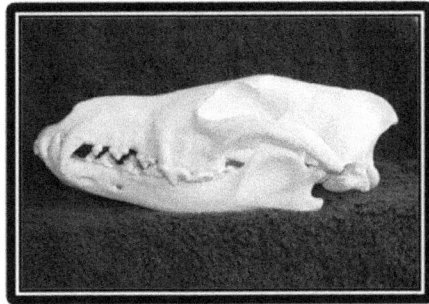

www.ingramcontent.com/pod-product-compliance
Lightning Source LLC
LaVergne TN
LVHW081323060426
835511LV00011B/1821